THE WORD

God's Last Word and Testament

About the Book

If you are a Christian you will have to wonder at the information provided in this book by God through his messenger, which will not be found in any other publication.

The doctrines and the very foundation of the Christian Church are challenged by God Himself and the sacraments are questioned as well as many other long held Christian beliefs.

Nevertheless, it does give the open-minded reader new insights into Christianity and religion that have not been written or expressed before, and in it God informs us of why we were born, the reason why we are here on earth and what is in store for us once we depart from this world.

It will give you, the reader first hand knowledge of what to expect and what you will be doing after you depart this life. Many of you who do not believe in life after death or reincarnation will be challenged in your beliefs and find that yes, indeed, you have lived many times before.

You will also find that God provides us with personal guidance from departed relatives and friends that are in spirit as well as providing help from a range of angelic helpers of all types.

There are also people on earth who are able to communicate freely and on a personal basis with all of those in spirit and the angelic world. These people are "spiritual messengers," and are not to be confused with spiritualists, psychics or mediums who play a different role and may hold different beliefs altogether.

About the Author

As a spiritual messenger, God has provided me with the ability to communicate directly with him and I have been speaking to him daily since the beginning of the year 2000.

In 2001 God asked me to write a book for him called 'The Word' and impart the following information to the world, which was and is to be his last testament to us before the final judgment. However as I had not attended church since early childhood or held any strong religious convictions, he advised me to study theology first.

As the contentious information God imparted to me had little relationship to what was being taught at theological college, it took me ten years to decide whether to share any of this material with the general public or not as I felt it would be offensive to many.

Also, I was more than a little concerned if not skeptical about some of the prophecies I was given until one after the other, they started coming true; so then, with a strong reminder from God about my covenant with him, I finally agreed to finish writing His book.

Therefore, I am writing these words on behalf of our Father who lives in heaven and who is giving me this information as I write. His name in Hebrew is YHWH, which is pronounced YAHWEH in English. Yahweh is calling his work 'The Word' and he says,

"I AM THE WORD!"

THE WORD

God's Last Word and Testament

Lee Anthony Looby PhD

Malakh House

2012

Malakh House
Mentone Victoria 3194 Australia
Copyright © Lee Looby 2009
Proof printed by Solutions Digital March 2009
Published 2012

National Library of Australia
~ Cataloguing in Publication Entry ~

Looby, Lee

The word: Gods last word and testament.

Bibliography

ISBN 978-0-9806232-2-2 (pbk)

Prophecy---Christianity

Word of God (Theology)

Dowey Number: 231.745

Other titles by this Author:

Interviewing Guardian Angels: With comments from God and Archangels.

Mentone: Malakh House, 2006.

Ω

Non-Fiction

English (United States)

Lulu Press Inc.

October 2012.

~

CONTENTS

FOREWORD

On Easter Sunday in 1986, at approximately 4:30 AM, I woke up due to a feeling of discomfort in the back of the neck, as though my head had lolled over the end of the bed and was unsupported.

Still half asleep, I tried to maneuver into a more comfortable position, as I was lying on my back. Both hands were resting on the bed beside me but I could not feel the bed beneath me. I soon realized that my body was floating about six inches above the bed, my head and arms unsupported with my hands resting on the bed.

As well as levitating, I found that except for my hands and head, I could not move. To further add to the weird situation, there were two strange "people" in the room speaking to each other.

Even though movement was limited, I could see a male figure on my right hand side standing next to me and another older male sitting on a wooden chair on the right hand side of the doorway.

When the two strange visitors realized I was awake, the one standing beside the bed started to speak to me. During the next twenty to thirty minutes he told me that I was not to renew my six year term of engagement with the Air Force when it expired, under any circumstances, and my destiny was to be that of a "spiritual messenger."

After elaborating on my future role as a messenger, he expressed how disappointed he was in me for wasting my time in the military.

After chastising me and reinforcing all that was said several times, they both promptly left. At that stage I found myself lowered back onto the bed, and being in peak physical condition, sprang out of bed after them, but as half expected, could find no one.

This levitation was deliberate and controlled. Whoever they were, the visitors were able to make my body defy the force of gravity. Not only could they do that, they could temporarily paralyze most of my body so that I was immobilized for the duration of the visitation and lecture.

The back door of the house was locked from the inside and was still locked when I checked. The large old fashioned key was still in the lock. The strong feeling of wellbeing was also unusual. For the next half an hour I experienced a sense of euphoria that I had not ever felt before.

This encounter led me to find out as much as I could about the spirit world and angelic beings. Even though it took me over five years of trying before I could make direct contact, I found I could communicate directly and freely through automatic-writing which finally led to a more personal communication through telepathy.

Utilizing both the skills of auto-writing and telepathy, I found I was able to call upon any angelic being or spirit entity at will and hold a conversation with them, and finally in the year 2000, I was also able to communicate directly with God.

To achieve this I had to pass several tests set for me over a period of forty days and nights by the angelic messengers, and after successfully passing all of them I was told that I had reached a level of spiritual awareness that would enable me to speak to Him.

I began to wonder what "spiritual awareness" actually was and what being a "spiritual" person really meant as the definition most people have of being a spiritual person is that the person is in pursuit of personal "enlightenment" which is only gained from self discovery found through years of solitude, meditation and prayer.

"Yahweh, what does it mean when a person says he or she is spiritual?"

"Lee, let me say that being Spiritual is my being available to you at any time and any place whatsoever, and if you are in touch with me every day, and you are with me every day then you are a spiritual person."

From this response we see that if a person is truly spiritual, it is perceived from the eye of God and not from the eye of the person. A person cannot say, "I am spiritual" or "he/she is spiritual," as whom, apart from God, can say who is truly spiritual? Therefore "spiritual" is defined as being high in the mind of God and angels.

INTRODUCTION

Throughout the ages, prophets; scribes, scholars; academics, theologians and other interested parties have collectively written down millions upon millions of words in the name of God.

The words written here are written with authority from firsthand knowledge of God, and from God, not from any human mind or any other terrestrial source at all. There will be no arguments put forward in this work to justify anything stated, just the plain facts as laid out in front of me, for you to either digest or discard as you see fit.

It is easy to write a story to match an event later with hindsight but not so easy to write a story with any accuracy before the event has happened, unless you are truly a prophet of God gifted in prophecy.

In Biblical times the prophet's stories were usually written down and recorded years after the events prophesied had actually happened, if they ever did happen; by paid scribes, and the stories were usually passed down by word of mouth through the generations; changing ever so slightly with each individual person's telling over their lifetime to suit their own religion, theology; ideology, position; social status, perception and intellect.

Early theologians, not prophets, have translated the Bible; and from that they have taken the liberty of editing the many stories to suit their own theology, based on their own indoctrination; beliefs and understanding so that the interpretations we now have are so grossly distorted from the original meaning that many are unrecognizable, even to God; leading to this, his last word and testament before his coming kingdom is upon us.

To add to the confusion, the many differing interpretations over the centuries have led to divisions on a multiple scale worldwide so that consensus on any passage among Christians, especially in relationship to the New Testament is now practically impossible to reach even on the most basic points.

Today many scholars and theologians are so bent on arguing and critiquing each others ideas and perceptions of the multiple interpretations, that common sense is left far behind and historical fact and truth seemingly fade into oblivion.

This work is different in that it was written before any foretold events in the future will have taken place and it is written by the living God directly through me, his earthly messenger, to restore this lost truth.

The words you are going to read here are the true and authentic words of the living God, not second-hand words or hearsay; nor are they written down centuries after the event but are written down by the hand of God who has literally taken hold of my hand in his own and written the words directly onto these pages in Melbourne, Australia. I have finally released them for publication in 2012, after taking ten years off to study theology and metaphysics in an attempt to understand all facets of this strange phenomenon.

There is only one reference to auto-writing in the Bible, where God took the hand of his Son and auto-wrote through him to impart a message to the people, though to date nobody has realized that this is what was actually happening at the time. The following words are this reference.

> 'But Jesus bent down and started to write on the ground with his finger. When they kept on questioning him, he straightened up and said to them, "If anyone of you is without sin, let him be the first to throw a stone at her." Again he stooped down and wrote on the ground.'
> (John 8: 6-8) NIV

The words coming through this messenger right now may be the only authentic words written down by God since that time. That is why this publication has no comprehensive bibliography, as all the words are original; not taken from the ideas of other men or women who have written each others words down to emphasize their own points of view, trying to argue against or validate them; but taken directly from the hand of the living God who is giving us these truths to digest.

All is authentic and all is directly from the living God who is here right now to give you this in writing himself, not from the mouths of biblical scholars but by the hand of the almighty God who has decided to give you a personal interpretation of this, his own Gospel to instruct you with.

God has been absent since his Son Jesus died, but now is back. Since his Son was crucified he has taken leave of the earth and all its inhabitants, to rethink and revise his plans. Having done that, he is here once more to implement those plans.

Some of you who are more astute than the general multitude may have noticed that the world has changed dramatically since the beginning of this, the 21st century. Let it remain then that the changes you see will be much more dramatic in the coming weeks, months and years to follow.

From what God has already personally imparted to me, today we are living in a religious fantasy made into our own reality by the figurative use of metaphor, rhetoric and hyperbole to explain the inexplicable. This has to be addressed and he has instructed me to tell you the truth in this, his Gospel, 'God's Last Word and Testament.'

"In the beginning was the Word, and the Word was with God, and the Word was God." (John 1:1)

"In the end is the Word, and the Word is with God and the Word is God." (YHWH 1:1)

THE WORDS OF THE LIVING GOD

"Let me begin by stating I am the living God who is here to tell you about myself, and I am going to tell you all you wish to know. I am giving my messenger permission to tell this to you now as you will need to know and it is important to you, and it will be more important later than it is now though you may not realize it just yet.

"Let it be seen that this work is the work of God Almighty who is here to tell you the truth, and the truth is that you are my sons and daughters and that you were created by my thought, not by chance and not invented by any other means other than what destiny has provided you with in your times.

"And these times are times of troubles and woes; so-be-it and so be the troubles which will always be with us to the end of days, and these days are not too far away.

"My Son is here too and we will soon be on earth to show all people that we are the Father and the Son and we are true and not fictitious; and we have been truth and life and we have shown the way to millions. And we are still finding people who are to be saved from the second-death which will overtake most of the human race.

"My Son lived on earth as a human being in the flesh. He died on the Cross and was taken off, laid in the tomb of Joseph of Arimathea and was dead and buried in this tomb.

"My Son was dead and buried when I sent an angel to breath life into his body [3.00 AM in the morning] and his soul returned to the fleshly body, [resurrected] but it was an agony for him and so I anaesthetized his body to make it non-feeling. And it was healing by itself, not by my hand but by its own natural healing processes.

"And he stank terribly and the stench was dreadful and the flesh was rotting so I made him stay away from human contact until the blood had circulated and the flesh had adhered to the bones and the breath was not fetid and the body was replenished with food and he had passed his wastes to rid the body of poisons and toxins.

"And he bathed and washed his wounds until they were clean and stopped bleeding. And then in this state he saw Mary who was told not to touch him and he was not to be touched until his fleshly wounds had recovered by exposure to the open air and he was clean again.

"Let it remain to be told that my Son died and was buried in the tomb designated for Joseph of Arimathea's parents. And Joseph was significant in the Jewish temple as a leader of the Sanhedrin, not just a member, but a chief priest, who believed that Jesus was more.

"And the Sanhedrin, priests and scribes were constantly arguing over Jesus' power of love and his power of healing and they heatedly contested that he was the Messiah.

"And they would argue incessantly over his decidedly superior powers and were furious that their leader believed in my Son's superiority so much, that Joseph allowed his body to be stored in the tomb designated for his own parents."

"What else can you tell me that is still unknown about the burial and resurrection, Yahweh?"

"The Sanhedrin cast a vote and then told Joseph to have this perceived imposter removed from his tomb at first light, thus creating problems for the mourners in that they had to take him to another burial site.

"And that is what the women were doing at the tomb at first light. It was still dark and so the image of my Son was not clear to Mary who first saw him."

[Once it was clear it was he she ran and told the others who rushed down the hill to see his body in the flesh, alive once more. But by the time the disciples arrived he had gone.]

"At first Mary thought the man she saw was a gardener due to the inexplicable appearance of Jesus to her at this time, and she later wondered how it came to be that she thought this, as no gardener would work before first light, and none were hired to keep the tomb free from overgrowing weeds or to rake leaves away from there."

"Yahweh, in the Gospel of Matthew, it says there was a violent earthquake and then an angel of the Lord rolled the stone away and sat on it." (Matthew 28:2)

"Lee, the stone had been rolled out of the way by the Sanhedrin to accommodate the transportation of the body out of there by the disciples who had been instructed to remove the body that morning.

"That is why the women had more spices; to anoint the body once more as it had already been attended to abundantly at burial, but now due to the pending reburial, all had to be ceremoniously done again.

"The disciples were prepared to take the dead body out of Joseph's tomb after the women, Mary and her helpers had re-anointed the body with oils and aromatic herbs used for this purpose. And this purpose was to keep the body fresh enough to make visitations possible, or in this case transportation from one burial site to another.

"The Roman guards were there in full view of all of it and none slept at all as it was punishable by death to sleep on duty, so none dared sleep. They were to be paid a large sum of money to tell any who asked that the disciples of Jesus came and removed his body at first light.

"My angels appeared to the Roman guards and spoke to them saying, 'The Lord Jesus is risen,' and the guards were told to report this to the Sanhedrin as well as to the Roman Curator.

"The guards reported it but were bribed by the Sanhedrin to say the disciples took the dead body away for reburial as scheduled. The disciples were ordered by the Pharisees to say this too.

[The reason the guards were told to say the body was stolen by the disciples was to deny he rose and to deny that the Sanhedrin knew anything about the pending removal which was scheduled for that morning.]

"When my Son appeared to the disciples in the upper room he had been waiting for them there. And he had put himself in a place unseen as he had not yet fully recovered and then made an appearance from behind the curtain after listening to their tales of woe.

"And he heard they loved him and he wept too. He appeared to them because he was feeling sad that they wept and they were all talking about him to each other."

[The curtain was at the entrance and there was a place, an alcove beside the door that was set apart for the people to put their goods and chattels and for women to place jars of water after entering the main room.]

"And Jesus was positioned behind this curtain and hidden from view until he could no longer contain himself. And he longed for their company so appeared to them all in a fleshly body and ate cooked fish with them to show them he was not a spirit but a living person.

"In their grief they had not considered he would be waiting there and they did not expect him to be there so did not search. And in their grief and joy and mixed emotions they wondered how he came to be there.

"And as it was dark in the room they were at first unsure it was he, as Jesus had lost weight due to dehydration and looked much older and different in the lamp-light of late evening.

"Jesus lived among his family, friends and disciples for forty days until he decided he was finished with this mission and wanted to return home. And I lifted his visible spirit into the air and he came home to me in spirit. And he left his earthly body in the holy place that I had prepared for it.

"And he became spirit once more to be able to enter my house as no flesh and blood can enter here."

"Yahweh, can you tell me what actually happened to the physical body of Jesus once his spirit left his body?"

"Yes Lee, I will tell all of you that no human body is capable of life out of the earth's environment and all spirit life is beyond the boundaries imposed on life, living on earth. The physical body of my Son was discarded as all bodies are at death and it was left on the earth to be returned to the earth as all bodies are.

"My Son is living now and he has been living intermittently on earth in the flesh and in spirit as he has reincarnated several times since his crucifixion. My Son has been able to tell me many things about human behavior and he has informed me of all the woes and troubles that have befallen my people since that time.

"My Son rose in spirit to be with me and he was alive again for forty days before coming home. He died on the day of crucifixion and rose to life again in the same body he left on the cross. And he rose for the reason of showing all of you that life lives on in spirit and can be returned to the body if the body is able to support it.

"My people saw it firsthand in the flesh and they remember it well. The Sanhedrin knew it was true and the disciples certainly knew as they were witnesses to this resurrection.

"My first impressions of this atrocity were too difficult for me to take in. And it was in vain that I sent him to deliver man from sin. And they destroyed their only chance to redeem themselves from death and were too ignorant of my plans to listen to reason. My plans were ignored and the multitudes won their right to take his life.

"My angels were not going to allow it to take place but my Son ruled that out by telling them it would be for the best, and it was as all eventually heard about his resurrection.

"My Son lived in the same body that he was born in after his crucifixion and then returned to me in spirit leaving his earthly remains behind for burial by his disciples.

"The story written and found in the Bible of him rising into the air was to give him supernatural status and to stop the Romans from finding and displaying the body. Let me state that hundreds of people witnessed seeing him living on earth for the forty days that he came back to life.

"And he was able to die in dignity after that as he was ready to leave his earthly body and return to me in spirit. His life was predestined for the event of becoming the Messiah, leading the Jewish people out of Roman hands. And it was not to happen as the Jewish leaders themselves denied his status and told the Romans they wanted him put to death, which they did.

"My Son is coming back to earth again in his full glory and he will be back to resume his role as savior of mankind. And he will be in the uniform of the day; that is, dressed as man dresses in the daytime in this day and age.

"And he will be distinguished by the markings that are on him and he will show the people that he has these distinguishing marks that are there to identity him. And they are not scars of crucifixion but are works created by artists in the manner of personal art.

"My Son will advise you of what he wants you to do, and you will listen if you want the best advice. My Son will advise you what to choose and he will ask you if you want to be left behind or be in front of the rest by telling me that you love me and want to come into my house and be with me, forever.

"My Son knows how important it is to be saved and he knows how much you want to live without fear of dying or fear of losing someone you love.

"Let it be seen that all people will have equal opportunity to come home to me, and all children will find it very easy to live here with me as I love my children and I will help them as much as I possibly can.

"Let me tell you too that I have begun to ascertain which of you is worthy of being in my house and which of you is to be discarded. My angels keep track of all you say and all you do, and report it back to me who listens with intent and hears about your life in minute detail."

"Yahweh, I have been told by a representative of the Jehovah's witnesses who knocked on my door in the year 2001 that Moses said in the Bible all forms of spiritism are an abomination to the Lord. (Deuteronomy 18:10-12)

"If this is the case, am I breaking your laws and if so, why am I able to speak to you as well as your heavenly messengers and all other spirit entities?"

"Lee, I have been waiting for you to ask me this and I am going to give you the reasons why you are not doing the wrong thing by communicating with spirits.

"You are my earthly messenger and you have the power to rebuke spirits! You are my anointed messenger who has the authority to speak to spirits!

"The ones who delve into the dead can be misled and become involved with rituals and practices that are unholy and that is why I have declared it not to be allowed, for that reason only and for those people only. And this was written in the Bible through my prophets and my messengers, who said these things.

"Your life has evolved in dealing with spirits and your life has been involved in dealing with evil and your life has been involved in helping lost souls and interrogating spirits who have sinned. And your life is now involved with the writing of my word so that others can find what they need to know.

"And the Bible was written for people of another era and times have changed. And the Bible was written by people with biased opinions though the Bible is my book of truths for the faithful. And I let all have the book of truths to read as they will be saved if they follow my word and my book.

"My book has been written by people and the words were reinterpreted to suit whatever they felt was right and whatever they thought they should write on my behalf without the knowledge of what they were writing.

"And the Bible has many anomalies that are not to my liking but at least people are reading it and at least people are listening. And people cannot be taken into the Abyss by *not* talking to spirits.

"So I have left it up to the discretion of the people who read the Bible to decide for themselves what I want them to do and what they do is their own business!

"Please realize that I have hold of the people's minds and if I wanted no-one to speak to the spirits I would not allow them to as I have the power to do this. And I also have the power to allow them the visions they have and I also allow them to hear the spirits, and I also allow them to believe in spirits as I am a spirit instead of a physical being.

"I want people to understand that if I am a spirit then other spirits are also here and they are able to contact them. And they can contact me if they are genuine and I will respond to them if they are responsive to my will.

"I can communicate with any if I want to, and I am a spirit, and I am the living God who created all things.

"So why do religious people say that it is against my rules to speak to spirits when I am a spirit? And why do they say it is wrong to communicate with the spirits who are telling them about future events as I give instruction to you who works as my messenger? (See Deuteronomy 18:18-20).

"Angels are also spirits and the guides are also spirits and the dead and the demons are also spirits and lost souls are also spirits and aliens are also spirits and the other entities that have been formed by thought are spirits; and all manner of entities are spirits!

23

"And therefore all are able to communicate with each other and all are able to communicate with the living and all are able to communicate with me if I so desire and all are able to speak their minds if they want to.

"And you are also allowed to speak your mind and you are also allowed to communicate with whomever you please, whether they are wicked or not.

"And whether they are wicked or not does not make you wicked nor does it make me wicked as I created them; so why would it be against my rules to allow you to speak to all of those I created?

"And why would I allow you to speak to some and not allow you to speak to others as if you were a common thief or a prisoner? And you are neither!

"I love you so do not let any religious sect frighten you out of speaking to me who created you. And I will punish them if they create problems for me!

"And I will punish them that tell you that you are not a true Christian by communicating with me, the true God and the living God and the only God; and the God of all there is, all that ever was, and all there ever will be!

"Let all know my word as it is your duty to tell them and I am going to elaborate on the information that I have provided to you in confidence. And if you feel it to be in your capacity to write these words of mine down for all, then please do so as you will have my blessings. And I will provide you with the time and the money to do my work as I provide all things to all people.

"And my reasons are my own and I want all to know that the rich and the poor are the same in my eyes. And I give more to those less and less to those more and this is to bring about a harmony that would not otherwise be, as those with less have more and those with more have less."

"Yahweh, I know what you mean but are we all going to be able to understand what you are telling us?"

"Lee, forgive me, I do not mean to be hard to understand and I will try my best to make all understood, and this will be in plain simple language for all to read and understand.

"And anybody anywhere who faithfully reads my word will know precisely what I mean unless they deliberately twist it around to suit their own ideology as has happened in my sacred book, the Bible.

"And that is why I am giving the people this as this is the new Bible and it is directly from me to the people through you, my beloved messenger. And I will be forever praising your efforts as I know how much you wish this cup to be taken from you.

"And I know how difficult this is for you and I know you are my faithful servant, and I know that you are doing this for me to help

25

your brothers and sisters gain everlasting life, as I have told you.

"And I have told you many things that I have not told anybody else, and you can now tell all as I want you to if you want to. So go ahead with it and then you will be finished with this, my word.

"I am letting you write this to give the people hope and to let my faithful know that I have not forsaken them, and that all of those who worship me in my churches are heading toward me. I do not differentiate between my churches as all lead toward me and they are all singing my praises, all that believe in me."

"Yahweh, none of these churches are teaching the truth as you have told me and are misleading the people, so why do you still want them to be part of the kingdom of heaven?"

"Lee, the reason is that they know the truth as it has been told to them and they are not to be forsaken for being misled. Only those who know that my Son died for them and turn their back on him, and do not want to consider me will not be able to enter the kingdom of heaven."

"Yahweh, does this mean the religions that do not acknowledge your Son are not true religions and these people will not be saved?"

"Lee, this means that people who are told about my Son and do not believe will not be allowed into my personal house, but all who have not been taught about my Son and die or have died without knowing about him will be considered on their merits."

"Yahweh, you are the God of the Hebrew people, yet they turned away from your Son; what is your intention with them now?"

"Lee, the truth is that all my people are allowed to enter my kingdom when they are reunited with me in heaven when they die and the House of Higher Learning is where they will be instructed.

"And the ones who do not make it to the House of Higher Learning will remain in a house suitable for them and they will not be part of my major plan."

"Yahweh, some religious people say that you are both the Father and the Son. Is this true?"

"I Am that I Am and my Son is my Son! I have not told any that I am also my Son and my Son has not told any that he is me! So how is it that some say this?"

"I think it may be due to indoctrination, misunderstanding or misinterpretation of the written word Yahweh, as I have no answer otherwise. These religious people quote from (John 10:30) NIV where Jesus says, 'I and the Father are one.'"

"Lee, I am not the Son and the Son is not me!"

"Would you like to elaborate on that please, Yahweh?"

"Yes, the Son has a life of his own and the Father has a life of his own and both have separate lives and both have different ideas and lead different lives."

"Yahweh, what did Jesus mean when he said, 'I and the Father are one?'"

"My Son meant we are identical in thought pertaining to moral teachings, and we are identical in many ways but we are different in that we are separate entities and have different lives to lead."

"Yahweh, what do you mean then when you say, 'I am the Word?'"

"Lee, the terminology is correct and it has been seen that people take it literally that I am my Son in the flesh. I am the creator and all that is on earth and in heaven is made by me, the God who is omnipresent and the God of all things great and small. My presence is in all that I have created and I am present in you as well as in the next person.

"My presence however is not of the earthly presence you think of and it is a spiritual presence not seen, but in the body, anyway.

"Without my presence in you there is no way you could live and breathe as it would be an inanimate body without any driven force to bring it to life, and it would be as a rock that has no thought or feeling.

"My presence in you is my Holy Spirit and that is why you can think and breathe independently and have mobility as without it you are dead. My Holy Spirit is in you when you live on earth, and when you die you are in spirit but without my life force in you, as your body is the temple for my Holy Spirit and you are therefore waiting to gain my Holy Spirit in heaven to attain everlasting life, and without my presence in you, you cannot ever attain that.

"That is why, when you attain everlasting life you are to be given a new body to live in.

"Let me tell you now that without the presence of my Holy Spirit in you there is no life force. And all living creatures as well as trees and plants have my presence in them."

"Yahweh, what do you mean when you say you are omnipresent?"

"Thank you for asking me Lee, as many people interpret this as meaning I am everywhere at once. That is not possible. I will elaborate on that. My presence is in one place, and that place is in my personal house known as the Kingdom of God.

"From my house I can hear everyone who is speaking my name and this is what I listen for. I can hear anyone speaking anywhere from my house. I can respond to anyone anywhere from my house.

"I am not everywhere at all times, rather I am in my house at all times and can hear many people speaking to me at the same time. I give preference to those in my favor and those not in my favor are not heard, until they are in my favor.

"My presence is like that of a spirit and my presence is felt rather than seen. My presence is felt even from my house and I give this feeling through thought and thought alone. My thoughts are heard and felt. My presence is in all my thought. My presence is not in my people physically. My thoughts are in my people.

"Lee, it will be understood in detail when it is experienced; and to experience my thoughts in your mind as you do, you must be at a high level of spiritual awareness."

"Yahweh, what then is the Trinity?"

"Lee, the Trinity is what the church calls me, my Son and my Holy Spirit. And my Holy Spirit is that part of me I send to all who are living to give to them the life force in their body and for healing of the body."

"Can you define that a little more, Yahweh?" It is like saying the Trinity is you and your Son; and your Holy Spirit whom you developed from your creativeness, to create life in others."

"Yes, my thoughts are what create new souls and they are formed from my energy which produces them. And they are from my thoughts that they are made and all who are made and all living things and all living creatures are produced like this and are manifestations of my thoughts."

"Yahweh, are you telling me that the Holy Spirit is also a thought, or one of your thoughts and that you and the Holy Spirit are one and the same?"

"Exactly, and my thoughts are continuous so I am continuously creating new life. My Son is my most wonderful creation and he is the greatest helper that I have ever created."

"Yahweh, is it possible for us as humans to create new life from our own thoughts?"

"Lee, it is, and you do it now though these basic thought forms which have substance, have no physical body but manifest as positive or negative energy and they are everywhere."

"What happens to these thought forms of energy we create then, Yahweh?"

"They are all in the astral plane and they live in the astral plane where you travel in your dreams and you see all of these forms in your dreams. And they are the ones who give you nightmares and they are the ones who bring good things to you and they are the ones who bring bad things to you, depending on the purpose for which they were created.

"And they live until they are negated and they are negated by an energy field which encompasses them as I rid the astral plane of them continuously, and the astral plane is not restricted to the earth plane."

"Yahweh, I have heard people criticize you, saying that while five hundred children die of starvation every hour, a football team wins a game after praying to you for a victory; why is this?"

"Lee, I give life not take it and the children starve and die because of mismanagement by men, not by me. And I provide ample for all people to live in abundance. It is the way people decide to live in your society and this is a democratic society that does not care for other less fortunate people who are unable to feed and clothe themselves, so they die.

"Let me state emphatically that if men treated each other as they treat themselves, starvation simply would not happen. I provide enough for every living soul to survive on and my angels help the world by overseeing that the food chain is constantly replenished.

"My angels are here to help mankind, not hinder, and they are constantly working to oversee the survival of all they can.

"My plan to create has flourished and all species are given an overabundance of seed to reproduce. And if all seed were sown then all living on earth would not be able to see each other through the thicket. Many perish in nature and so it is with man. I make sure that man survives and man does the rest. If man fails man then it is his fault, not mine."

"Yahweh, did you make man apart from the rest of nature, I mean is man made specifically to rule over all the earth?"

"Yes, man is provided with enough intellect to be in charge of his environment. And he should look after it; and if not, he will perish.

"To argue that I do not care about the dying children is wrong, and the reason I give all souls the opportunity to live again is that they are not proven to live in my house until they have reached adulthood and shown me they are worthy. Then and only then will I consider them for everlasting life in my house.

"My own house is my personal space for my own children who have been forgiven of any wrong doing and have shown me they are truly decent souls. My only way of seeing if they are the truthful and kind souls they are meant to be is to test them.

"One life is not enough and if a child dies then he has not lived long enough to prove his worthiness. My plan is to create more than is. To create more than is, I will need trustworthy helpers to provide for the new worlds and new life I want them to make for me.

"To think I am stupid enough to let a child die without living again is beyond my comprehension. And it annoys me that people blame me for these childhood deaths and berate me. You will all see my plans in action when you arrive here to look at all you have achieved over many life times. Then you will understand.

"When men have learned to manage their resources and are not blinded by greed and profit, five hundred children every hour will be fed and clothed, not put into circumstances beyond their control and die.

"And when this happens people will feel more for each other, and at present this is to be seen only when they find themselves in critical circumstances.

"My angels provide help for those who pray. And the football team is helped by the angels who provide hints for them by projecting their thoughts into the minds of the players, showing them how to get the winning goals. And that is why they win. When people pray to me my angels promptly respond as they can do many things to help."

"So, saying a prayer does help, Yahweh? I have heard of people who have prayed for help, and nothing ever happened for them."

"Lee, of course prayer helps and if it is in earnest and not for personal gain, my angels try to provide the help asked for. The issue of starving children will be addressed when more and more people working in my name start helping them and feeding them.

"My angels are constantly helping the starving children with life giving necessities, though they are not able to accommodate all of them yet; as they have too much to do, just trying to keep up to the incongruous situation worldwide, where the rich deprive the poor of food by selling it at a high price and dumping whatever is not sold.

"When man becomes more compassionate, only then will they behave in a loving manner toward their starving children and save their lives. Unless man becomes more generous in every way then I cannot help with the problems they have created for themselves."

"Can man learn to become more compassionate, Yahweh?"

"Lee, all men are born with this instinct to provide for the lesser members of society and this is taken away by self interest. When it becomes necessary, men will revert to helping each other.

"When mankind becomes more interested in saving the human race from extinction, they will distribute the food supplies properly to keep themselves going and let the children have enough to eat to sustain them, as food will be in great shortage everywhere."

"Thank you Yahweh, now to bring up another contentious issue. What do you think of women being ordained as clergy in the Christian Church?"

"Lee, it is acceptable in my eyes and it is not to be turned into a matter of conjecture as it is the word and it is the way and it is the truth. And my truth is spoken through men and through women.

"Let me suggest that you write this down as well.

"I created men for the purpose of grooming and nurturing the earth; and to do this they have to reproduce. Therefore I created women with strong survival instincts whose main purpose was to reproduce and nurture the young, the sick and the elderly.

"Women are not chattels but were provided for men to have and to hold and to care for their children. And I made woman five-sevenths the stature and strength of a man. And they are now developing to their full potential and are able to carry on and help with the scientific and technical advances men have made.

"Women are quite capable of doing the work men can do and some have excelled in fields that are not regarded as women's work at all. And women are also excellent communicators and most can articulate their thoughts very well.

"And the tongue of a woman is capable of speech is it not? And the tongue of a woman has the same impact on the hearing as the tongue of a man, so why should church leaders say that women are not allowed to preach my commandments and speak in my name?"

"I think it is probably because of cultural differences, ego and arrogance, Yahweh. These men and most men believe that women are lesser beings than they are and see them as unclean as they menstruate and go through emotional hormonal changes every month; therefore church leaders think that women are not worthy of being given the role of speaking on your behalf."

"Lee it is true, and these men are wrong to say that women are less capable of speaking in my name and are made solely for the comfort of man; I made them primarily as a companion for man.

"And it is my will that all can speak on my behalf and it is my will that women are allowed to say whatever is on their mind and take part in politics, and take part in decision making."

"Thanks Yahweh, now that we are speaking about some delicate human issues, did you intend some people to be homosexual?"

"Let me tell you this Lee, I wanted all women to be able to carry children and I wanted all men to be able to father children; but things go astray and some are born unable to do this and some have other problems with health, and others do not want children."

"So it was not intentional that some people are homosexual, Yahweh?"

"Let me tell you that I created man and woman to be together with one another in the hope of having many, and it was not my intention to have man love man sexually; but somehow the genetics became varied and hormonal changes resulted from this, creating people of the same gender who are attracted to each other. And now it is recognized as an intricate part of their individuality, not a perversion as thought by most."

"Yahweh, what is your current opinion of homosexuality, then?"

"It is acceptable as you are aware that man is a many sided being and has many ways of expressing himself. And this is his way of expressing himself as you have a way of expressing yourself.

"And if you accept the way you express yourself why would you think that homosexual men and women would not accept the way they express themselves?"

"Yahweh, I'm sure they do but it is regarded as sinful in our society for them to be living together as homosexuals."

"Lee, is it sinful to eat? Is it sinful to wash? Is it sinful to speak?"

"No, not here in our democratic society in Australia where we have civil rights and freedom of speech."

"Well, then it is not sinful to partake of sex and I gave homosexuals this option. And it is the way that some men are born and it is the way some women are born.

"And some men use the left hand to write and this is not a sin. And some women use the left hand to write and this also is not a sin; so why do people regard this expression of sex as sinful?

"Let me go on and say that the ones born like this are not committing sin but the ones who have this way of life who are not homosexual but live in this fashion are sinning in my eyes."

"Yahweh, are you saying that it is a sin if a heterosexual man lies with another man but not a sin if a homosexual man lies with another homosexual man?

"I'm asking you this because Moses is quoted in the Bible, (Leviticus 18:22 & 20:13) and in other places as saying that homosexuality is an abomination and today it is also seen as a means of transmitting disease. These are the words Moses spoke so long ago."

"Do not lie with a man as one lies with a woman; that is detestable."
(Leviticus 18:22) NIV

"If a man lies with a man as one lies with a woman, both of them have done what is detestable, they must be put to death; their blood will be on their own heads." (Leviticus 20:13) NIV

"Lee, let me speak! I have told you my wrath is for heterosexuals who lie with those of the same sex! Although homosexuals are of the same sex as those they lie down with, this is the exception as they are born to lie down with their own type, not committing a sin in my eyes!"

"I'm sorry, Yahweh, I didn't mean to make you angry."

"Lee, it is important that no mistake is made here as in the past!

 "And I do not want one word altered or even one alteration without my permission!

"And the Bible was written by men for me on my behalf but some have put their own thoughts down instead of my thoughts!

"And the Bible has been written by men who wrote it many years after the events happened and the events were diminished in their living memories, and the translations are from one language to another!

"And then from that to the next has lost the meaning and all is translated to the beliefs of the person translating; so the finished article is not the article, and a lot has been discarded and a lot has been changed, and a lot has been misrepresented and a lot has been misinterpreted!"

"Thank you Yahweh, I'm sure that anyone reading this will get the general idea. Now I want to ask you about circumcision. Why did you create men with a foreskin if you want them to remove it?"

"The transmission of diseases such as Aids is limited if they listen to my teaching that all men should have the foreskin removed. And that is why I have told them to do this as it is in their best interest to do so!

"And it was seen as a way to allow them to take hold of themselves in the absence of a partner, and when I finally provided enough women for them this became a part of the body without a purpose, and it was also a protection for the glans (tip of the penis) before adequate clothing was worn.

"And it was for that reason I proposed this covenant with Moses as he asked me to have a way to prove to me men were following my Commandments, with a sign. And I asked him to carry out circumcision on the faithful who were my followers and had been in my sight and did my work, and were the sons of highly regarded men." (Yahweh made the original covenant with Abraham.)

"Yahweh, what did you mean when you said you finally made enough women for man? There are many more males born than females in our country and other countries, creating an imbalance."

"Lee, it is the survival of the fittest and the male who woos and wins the female to procreate with is usually healthier and wealthier than the one who is rejected and denied this pleasure. To provide for a wife takes time and effort and to compete for a woman, men must at least learn a trade and become productive.

"And it is to provide a family environment for women who need and require the secure family structure necessary for survival, due to the number of surplus males.

"At the time I made Adam, I had it in mind to make him a partner. After making Eve, I then made Adam more wives and I made them for him like I made him, from the earth; and he had sons and daughters from them too."

"Yahweh, in Australia we are told we are only to have one wife. You approved of Adam taking more than one wife. Why is that?"

"The reason is that Adam had children from several wives and those children then had their own children. The best results have come from a mixture of genes, and this greater genetic pool has provided a better chance for the human race to begin with."

"Yahweh, then it is acceptable to have more than one wife now?"

"Lee, cultural upbringing permits this to happen in many societies without bloodshed. And this is the way to keep all women fed and clothed in some civilizations where, if not for the support of the wealthier males, single women would find themselves destitute.

"In your egalitarian society there is no need for more than one wife as nearly[1] all women are now regarded as equal, are self sufficient and can work or receive support from the government.

"Let me tell you that in your society men in general do not want to be taken in marriage with a woman who only wants them for their money and their status. My plan is no longer working as you know men are now far less inclined to marry and have a family.

"Many men would prefer to have multiple partners and have this lifestyle without the responsibility of rearing a family under one roof with one partner, as it would make them feel obliged to conform."

"Yahweh, theologians have told me that the name Adam is a term used for early mankind and is not just the name of one first man."

"Lee, these people are too far removed from the facts. As you know they are unaware of who actually wrote my words down and the more they seek the answers to this the more confused they become.

"My Adam was indeed the first specimen of his kind as one man. He was the first man and I did not have an assembly line. Each person was born in turn one after the other and one from another and that is the reason why Adam had more than one wife."

"Yahweh, do you approve of women being circumcised too?"

---

[1] Wage disparity, social inequity and racial discrimination.

"Let me begin by stating emphatically, No!

"Let me bring it to the attention of all who are intelligent enough to understand, that a woman reaches sexual orgasm from her clitoris and this is removed in female circumcision.

"Let me tell you that this is not only excruciatingly painful but makes that woman unable to have a relationship that has any sexual gratification, and that was not my plan.

"Let me give you an understanding that female circumcision has no place in our society and this is imposed on women by men who want to control them and prevent them from experiencing orgasm."

"Yahweh, can you tell us a little about yourself so that we may have an understanding of you and the life you lead?"

"Lee, I have been absent but am now back again. I have but one name, Yahweh, though man knows me by many names.

"My beloved Son calls me Dad, therefore, no name compares to Dad in my eyes!

"My Son's name was rendered from *Yeshua* in his native Aramaic tongue into the name Jesus in English. My Son has many names, though in English you know him only as Jesus."

The name Jesus is an <u>Anglicization</u> of the <u>Greek</u> Ἰησοῦς (*Iēsous*), itself a <u>Hellenization</u> of the <u>Hebrew</u> יהושע (*Yehoshua*) or Hebrew-<u>Aramaic</u> ישוע (*Yeshua or Y'shua*), meaning 'Yahweh rescues.'

"Yahweh, what do you mean by saying you '…have been absent, but am now back again?'"

"Lee, it is because I have been busy with other species similar to man and I have not been on earth for many centuries, leaving the work to my angels.

"And I want you to write this book to let all know my words are the only words and my thoughts are the only thoughts; and my writing is the final word, and this is the final word!

"And all who read and learn my final word will be the few who are with you and with me and my messengers on the last day of the world, as you know it.

"And you will be telling all who will listen to you the truth. And all who will not listen will not be allowed into my kingdom as I will not let them in as they have not believed me, and they have not listened to my final word.

"And they are to be left on the earth plane until they are either forgiven or redeemed by prayer by others who pray for their souls.

"And my word will then be heard for the truths! And my word will be

44

heard by the people who will then know! And my word will be the final word! And my word will be heard by all!

"And even the demons that are left in hell to perish will know my word before the end! And they will gnash their teeth in anguish for not listening. And they will wring their hands and beg for forgiveness! But alas, it will be too late to forgive them and they will perish!"

"Do you have any living children anointed by you and your Holy Spirit, Yahweh?"

"Yes, I have children on earth doing my work. And I have children on earth who are born of man and children on earth not born of man anointed by my Holy Spirit. And some of my messengers from the houses of angels not born of man but born of my Holy Spirit have been on earth doing my work.

"And some of my children now on earth as messengers are born of man and are blessed by my Holy Spirit.

"It is going to be the start of a wonderful life for all and it is going to be a time of great joy for all, and it is going to be a time of creation.

"And all of you will see many new things and all will be astonished at this, and all will be in awe of my works; and all will be in wonderment at my works, and you will be able to participate in it and partake of it all.

"And you will be able to enjoy it all and you will be rewarded for your life as my messenger. And you are the one I have anointed to do this."

"Yahweh, is it true Mary was a virgin, as I have read that the Hebrew word for virgin can be literally translated or interpreted as meaning an unmarried maiden?"

"My Son was born of my Holy Spirit and Mary was indeed a virgin, never having been touched by and never having lain with a man before my Holy Spirit was placed into her womb by me."

"Yahweh, what is the reason you let your only Son die on the Cross? Did he die for our sins or to prove to us life is everlasting?"

"His crucifixion was the start of my plan for mankind's salvation and I want all people to recognize his sacrifice and to let them know that I am here. And I have shown them that life is everlasting by letting him live again.

"And he raised Lazarus, brother of Mary and Martha, and the daughter of Jairus from her death; and a boy, the son of a widow in Nain from his funeral bier. And Jesus lived as he was raised from death on the Cross, and he was and is the living proof that I am the living God of Israel!

"And the Romans believed before the Jews, and the Jews turned their backs on him before the Romans who were more agreeable to his teachings than my own chosen people, who turned their face away from him and from me.

"My people can only come to me through him and if they do not believe he died and came back then they cannot believe in the kingdom of heaven and therefore will not be able to access my house in my kingdom, the Kingdom of God."

"Yahweh, you said you were no longer residing in the Jewish temple; what are your plans regarding the Jews now?"

"Lee, my people are the ones who killed my Son Jesus! My Son is my most wonderful asset to me!

"Let me say that he has been the most wonderful Son any father could ever wish to have and he has been the most wonderful man ever to live too.

"My love for him is unending and my plans are that eventually my people, the Jews that are saved, are to be here in my house ruling over the universe but with my Son in charge, and he will be and this is my pledge to them too."

"Yahweh, will any Christians be at the forefront of your Kingdom as well as the Jews?" [2]

"Let me remind you that Christians are relatively newcomers and my people are my own, so who is to be selected first?"

---

[2] Then I heard the number of those who were sealed: 144, 000 from all the tribes of Israel. (Revelation 7:4) NIV

"Let it remain to be seen that you have this in mind by the time the end times are upon you and it will be very soon, so be prepared for this and be prepared for the end times to happen too.

"And be told these times are going to be and you will see sign after sign that the end will soon be here, and so will all who believe.

"Let it be seen that the New Jerusalem will be here in my kingdom with my Son in the front seat, not the Rabbis or the Priests but my Son and his faithful followers.

"Let it be then that all have time to be faithful... have time to be forgiven... and come to me unencumbered, without guilt or debt.

"It is true and it will happen, so be ready for it and be the one to take credit for knowing it, as you will direct people to it all and you will be ready to help. And you will be ready to have your time in my house with me too.

"Let it remain to be seen that it will be my time out and my Son will be the one in charge of all of it, not just the country of your birth, but the whole planet.

"Let it be seen that to be ready for this event, all believers will understand my word and all will have knowledge of me and of my Son too."

"What is meant by the churches saying Jesus died for our sins then, Yahweh? Jesus himself said it was to forgive us of our sins."

"Lee, the churches add ceremony as they wish and make more than was intended to be. The message is clear that all who are free of sin will live forever with me in my house and all who are not free of sin, will not!"

"So, Jesus died to show us that there is everlasting life and not because of our past or future sins, or original sin Adam and Eve may have committed?"

"Lee, all sinners have the chance of being forgiven by asking."

"By asking personally or by having others pray for them, Yahweh?"

"All living sinners who ask for forgiveness and are genuine and have shown remorse and who are not going to sin again deliberately by making this a habit, will be forgiven.

"My Son died to show that he was the resurrection and the life and through him all may have that, and all may live again after death and all have been shown; and all who see and all who have been told and all who believe in me and my Son will see everlasting life!"

"He died for that reason, Yahweh?"

"Yes, he died for the reason of letting all know that life is everlasting and that the resurrection is a truth and that they too will be resurrected as my Son was resurrected to life, and they are to be resurrected if they are to be judged and all will be judged, so all will be resurrected."

"Yahweh, we are told in church and by other Christian evangelists that Jesus died to free us from the Original Sin committed by Adam and Eve, not as proof of everlasting life."

"Lee, the second death is the sentence I have imposed on all of mankind because of Original Sin!

"Let me explain! My Son died for mankind to release mankind from death! To be released he must be sin free! To have no sin he must be forgiven!

"To have my Son die for this reason was to give many people the chance to be sin free by asking for forgiveness of sin. Sin [here] is the personal sin of man, not the sin of Adam and Eve as you think.

"And I mean contemporary man, not original man and not Original Sin. Man was always destined to die the natural death he does today. Original Sin was the reason for the beginning of the second death in the heavenly body after death in the earthly body.

"Everybody has the same chance of being delivered from the second death by following my word and my way!

"Second death is a reality, not a myth! Second death is for those not acceptable to me in my house at the time of judgment!"

"Yahweh, earlier you said you were the God of Israel, does that mean the Israelites are the chosen people and all others are secondary in your eyes?"

"Lee the truth is much more difficult to tell you. And the people reading will become very upset to learn the truth about my people and why I prefer them over all the others.

"My people were those that I created from my own thought and when I was creating the heavens and the earth I created many helpers and watchers who were and still are spirit beings, not physical beings at all, and they were rewarded by being given the right to create whatever they wanted, and I allowed them to have that privilege, and they did.

"That is why the people on earth are so diversified and most races are now mixed and intermingled, bringing to a head the best of the genetic material available as many earlier races were wiped out because they were unacceptable to their own creators, and they have been extinguished altogether from the face of the earth.

"Let me tell you directly from my own mouth that all races were created by different designers and that they were the creation of my helpers. And that is why some are behind the rest of the world and why my own creations are ahead in the world."

> Then God said, "Let *us* make man in our image, in *our* likeness, and let them rule over the fish of the sea and the birds of the air, over the livestock, over all the earth, and over all the creatures that move along the ground." (Genesis 1:26) NIV

"The Israelites have spread themselves throughout the world and interbred with people from nearly every nation, bringing to the world new breeds of hybrid people that have traits from those not of my original design. My wish is to bring to the people a sense of equality, and they will find this eventually, but for now the other races are not equal in my eyes and are not loved as much by me.

"Why not, Yahweh?"

"Let me remind you that this is my truth here; let it be said that this discussion is not related to any other discussion before this.

"The breath of life in these human beings is imparted to them by the helpers who created their souls. My own people were created entirely by me and the breath of life was given to them by me personally. My Holy Spirit enters into them to bring life to them and that is the truth.

"The people not of my design are looked after by my helpers who created them, and my helpers are fully responsible for their own creations. The hybrids that are produced from the mixing of my own people and my helpers people are looked after spiritually by me.

"To fully grasp the implications of what is being said, all those human souls who eventually end up in my personal house after judgment will be given the freedom to create and they may even create worlds of their own and populate them with their own creations.

"It takes many millions of years to populate a planet, not six thousand years as some have interpreted six days as meaning.

"Even a blade of grass takes more than six days to grow, so how is it possible for me to create millions of species by myself and have them mature in only six days, followed by a seventh day of rest?"

"Yahweh, now I can see why the ancient Greeks and Romans referred to many gods in their epical stories and poems.

"Yahweh, when you created Adam, did you make him look as man does today or did he look like pre-historic Neanderthal man?"

"Lee, this is the only way to explain it. I created the primitive ape-like creatures long before I created humanity, and no human being alive today is a direct descendant from any of these species. And I made man far superior to Neanderthal man, and mankind is a different species.

"And to say man evolved from ape is stupidity. Apes were meant to be a different species and will always be, and they will not evolve any further. And to think the ape of today will eventually evolve into you, or another species or race of mankind is not correct.

"The Hebrew people were the ancestors of the historical, biblical Israelites, who came much later, and they were born as men and women; and they appeared then as they do today, not evolved from prehistoric man."

"Yahweh, when you created the helpers who in turn created most of the human race, did you create a personal helper for yourself?"

"Lee, I made man in my image and when I say man, I mean male and female. All living creatures and all spirit entities have companions and I am no exception. Let me explain this to you.

"Nearly all men need the comfort of a woman's love and require sex to live in complete happiness. Without a woman to love, lonely men would have an overwhelming and unfulfilled desire for sex.

"My decision to do this is now difficult to bear and I feel responsible for the disparity in sexual desire as women do not need sex to live happily whereas men do. I gave men a strong sex drive to keep them active and healthy, and to pursue women and provide for them. My plan was to have men need women for comfort and companionship, and women to need men for love and security.

"Let me tell you this too Lee, I have a companion and this will be hard for any of you to accept, but my companion is in the form of a woman and she is my own creation, not created for me by my helpers but created from my own thought; and my queen, the Queen of Heaven was the prototype for earthly women."

"Yahweh, I can see many skeptical readers throwing this book straight out of the nearest window right now."

"Let them, and men will throw out the women in their lives too as they are still human; and I made them for man to have, and they have them, don't they?

"This relationship in my world is entirely spiritual and has a much deeper substance to it than anything achieved on earth.

"This spiritual connection will by far be much more satisfying to you than any sexual encounter, so take it that life in my world will be far better than anything you have experienced on earth."

"Well Yahweh, it is a lot for a human to take in and many will not want to accept it, even if it is a spiritual relationship."

"Lee, then they will find life in my world much more difficult to adjust to and accept, as many things are not told to man on earth.

"And they will have to learn many things from my angels and adjust at the time of judgment. And this is one of the reasons they will have to progress through the five levels in the light before being allowed into my house.

"And let it be seen by scholars researching the scriptures that many passages referring to my companion have been scrupulously removed, not once or twice, but many times over."

"Yahweh, may we digress here as I would like some more information about the Israelites."

"Lee it will be fine to add more here about the Israelites. My people have been my pride and joy and in my eyes they are the most wonderful people in the world. And I say this because they think I am not thinking of their woes and are worried about this.

"And even though they have been praying to me in their synagogues they worry that I have left them behind. And it does appear that way as I have been absent from their temple for nearly 2000 years.

"My messenger Moses brought them the Ten Commandments and now today thousands of years later, my messenger is bringing over one hundred new ones. Not only is he bringing all of you new rules to abide by, he has been given the task of telling you about the seven spiritual realms in my world.

"The little book that is spoken of in the New Testament in the Revelation to John, (Revelation 10:2) my messenger has opened it and published it.

"And the people who have read it have been given new insights into my plans, especially for those who will make it into my realms. And they will be thinking differently about the kingdom of heaven after they have read it.

"And many of the disasters foretold in the Bible and by modern day seers have already happened. The spirits in my houses in heaven have no idea of the future either, and although I have given them some insights into the future, many have mistaken these events as insignificant disasters, overall.

"The events are not greater than the New Orleans flooding but they have impacted on hundreds of thousands of people in third world countries, though these are not seen as very important or even as fulfilling biblical prophecies, by the western world."

"Yahweh, it is apparent to a lot of people that these terrible disasters happening worldwide lately may be those mentioned in the Bible, prophesied as happening before the end times; and until recently, some of the world's leading politicians were even in denial over global warming, so how could they ever accept these events as being the ones Jesus spoke of?"

"Let me tell you this Lee, my Son provided enough information to allow believers to know what is really happening today. The politicians are not concerned as my plans are not their plans. Let it remain to be seen that they see the end times in the full light of day but not realize what it is that is in front of them.

"I have made their minds like wet cement and as cement dries out it becomes thicker and thicker until hard, and in this mind set the politicians will soon have no way of understanding anything that is of any importance or any value to anybody."

"Does the United States have to go through anymore major upheavals and catastrophes, Yahweh?"

"Let all know that the Unites States will take the brunt of my wrath and any citizen living there reading this, would be wise to leave."

"Yahweh, as the creator, are you going to destroy what you have created?"

"Let it be seen that my plans are not directly from my own hand but the hands of the angels who look after the planet. These angels always make corrections to allow the planet to thrive; and when I tell them to turn away from a particular disaster looming on the horizon, then there is nothing to stop that event happening; and that is how I make my retribution, by inaction rather than by action.

"My retributions will be in many forms and if you have read of the Exodus where Moses gave Pharaoh ten major plagues to deal with, know that the modern day Babylon will also have major plagues to contend with, bringing this den of iniquity to its knees."
(Exodus chapter 7 to chapter 12)

"Yahweh, are you telling me that the USA is really the Babylon spoken of in the Bible?" (Revelation, chapter 8 to chapter 19)

"Let me tell you that the USA is indeed the Babylon spoken of. The whole USA is symbolically the city spoken of as it is all united as one and has been one for well over two hundred years.[3]

"And now the people are all in the one united place, they call themselves Americans and they are all from one place, America, and this America is the 'Mother of Harlots' spoken of."
(Ref. Revelation 17:5)

---

[3] The United States Declaration of Independence was adopted on 4th July 1776.

EASTER DAY

"Yahweh, can we now speak about your Son when he lived in biblical times? The Church tells us that Jesus died on a Friday and was resurrected on the third day, though if he died at approximately 3:00PM on Friday afternoon and was raised up early on the Sunday morning, that is less than two days counting in hours; i.e., part of Friday, all of Saturday which was the Jewish Sabbath and only part of Sunday morning which was the first day of the week. (A new day started at sunset then.)

"That partly covers the three days as he was dead on the Friday afternoon, all of Saturday and part of Sunday morning, but the time frame only covers two nights. Jesus himself prophesied he was to be 'in the heart of the earth' for three days and three nights,[4] and some academics are now putting forward the idea that the Crucifixion may have taken place a day earlier than at first thought.

"If Jesus was to be crucified and buried before the Passover began that means he may have been Crucified on a Thursday afternoon before this special annual Passover began, rather than the Friday afternoon we call Good Friday, and this seems the easiest and most logical way to explain the three days and three nights 'in the heart of the earth' as foretold.

"Was Jesus actually crucified on a Thursday afternoon, fulfilling the prophecy of three days and three nights in the heart of the earth?

---

[4] (Matthew 12:40)

"According to the Law of Moses every Passover is followed by a Sabbath day of rest no matter what day of the week it falls on. For example, if the Passover falls on a Saturday the special Passover Sabbath would fall the next day on the Sunday; so the Sabbath for that Passover would be on the Sunday.

"And If Jesus was resurrected on this Sunday morning it was also a very special day for the Jews, being their Passover Sabbath."

"Lee, my Son died on the Cross on the Friday which is now considered by those who read the records as day one of death and Saturday, normally the Jewish Sabbath as day two of death and Sunday as the third day of death.

"And the majority of people at that time counted sundown in the evening of the preceding day they were in as the starting point of a new day, and therefore today it is taken by many people that the three days spoken of in the prophecy were fulfilled.

"However, my Son died in the afternoon on the Friday which was just prior to the normal Jewish Sabbath which started at sundown that day. As the Passover also fell on Saturday which was the Sabbath, another special Sabbath [the first day of the feast of unleavened bread] was held on the Sunday.

"And my Son arose the morning after the Sunday Sabbath which made it a matter of three days that he was in my house with me."

"So, Yahweh, this is where the discrepancy comes into it... Jesus used the sign of Jonah, of being three days and three nights in the belly of a whale as a prophecy to the scribes and Pharisees of being in the heart of the earth for three days and three nights.

"And all the other parables only mention three days, so the early church regarded the sign of Jonah as allegorical and only counted three days, when in fact three days and nights from the Friday take us to the Monday."

"Lee, let me remind you that the Jewish people held this Sabbath day in high esteem for the reason of the feast of unleavened bread which was a solemn time, and they took it with the Passover feast as the beginning of a good year, and it was this that prompted the early Church to first consider Sunday worship."

"Did the Christian church later establish having their Sabbath day on Sunday rather than Saturday out of respect for the resurrection of your Son as well, Yahweh?"

"This is truly the reason that Sunday is now the Christian day of worship rather than the Jewish Sabbath, and it is now thought by all Christendom that he rose on the Sunday morning.

"And my church of Christ now believes it is best to leave Sunday worship as it stands and not antagonize those who are involved in worshipping my Son, as he does not worry on which day you worship.

"And all the holiday festivals around this time are to be included in the time-frame for church services to be held, and placed in the minds of all to be remembered as the day of days, not the holiday of Easter but the holidays of Easter which include the Monday.

"Let me remind you too that after the Sunday Sabbath, this special Sabbath due to the annual Passover, my Son was resurrected the morning after, and this is the way to read it purely for the records.

"And this explains the three nights well enough for anyone to understand it, if they did not think he was in the heart of the earth for three days and three nights, whichever way you look at it.

"Read the scriptures properly and it plainly states that Jesus rose the morning after the Sabbath, and that Sabbath was the Sunday Sabbath and that Sunday Sabbath was an extra Sabbath."

"So, that means Jesus *was* actually dead and buried in the heart of the earth for three days and three nights, fulfilling the prophecy?"

"Yes Lee, my Son had a habit of ignoring Jewish protocol and breaking the rules. He made it difficult for all by rising after the special Sabbath reserved for religious ceremonies knowing that it was an extra special day in Jewish Law, and Law was more important to them than life itself, as without following the rules of the Law there could be no social interaction between the people and the traders in the synagogue."

"Thank you Yahweh, and now will you tell me in what year your Son Jesus was crucified and resurrected?"

"Lee, it was in the year 31 Anno Domini."

"Well that will astonish millions of people who have already pinpointed the time and date by researching the available data, Yahweh. Most have calculated that the crucifixion took place in 33 A.D. Interested people will now be looking at it again to calculate which day the Passover actually fell on in the year 31 A.D."

"Lee, even current researchers are convinced that it was in a time frame that coincided with many events written in the Bible, but the Bible was written many years after the resurrection happened, as all waited for the end times then and did not record it accurately."

"Yahweh, how did your Son get out of the shroud and other burial garments, then get dressed, as his hands and feet had just had large metal spikes hammered through them on the cross and a spear was thrust deep into his abdomen?"

"My angels were sent to look after his body to prepare it for the occasion and to put the sentries at their ease."

"Yahweh, what did the cross look like? Some theologians now think it was actually a tree or a log, not a man made structure."

"This was a timber structure made by practical means and it was a horizontal piece of timber eight inches by six inches, recessed and joined to another piece of recessed timber by crossing at right angles to the vertical. And it was constructed to suit the occasion.

"And this vertical piece of timber was over ten feet in length and it was ten inches by eight inches hewn from a tree and shaped by an adze and it was carried by my Son until he could not manage it."

"Yahweh, is the Shroud of Turin the true burial cloth of your Son Jesus?"

"Lee, it hurts me to think that people cheapen my Son by showing a cloth with an image imposed on it. The cloth was not worn by my Son and it has been misrepresented to all and has nothing at all to do with my Son."

"Yahweh, will Jesus be able to relate to modern man when he returns, and will he be able to convince the people he is the real Messiah, not just one of many self proclaimed Messiahs who will try to fool the elect?"

"Let me tell you truthfully Lee, My Son lives on earth with your people and he is very up to date with the modern world and all of the modern technology. Many will come in his name and many will be deceived, though no-one will mistake him as his presence will be like no other on earth, and his authority will be directly from me."

"Thank you Yahweh, now, can we change the subject for the time being and go onto some other topic of interest?"

"My Son is more important to me than any other topic but if you need a break from this subject, then I am ready."

YAHWEH THE CREATOR

"Did you create the universe, Yahweh?"

"Yes, I am the creator of all that is in existence. And I am the being who created all that ever was in existence, before any. And I became the creator from the gases of the unknown, and I became who I am because of this.

"And I became the creator of all living creatures and all the dead souls. And I create new souls everyday, and I extinguish those souls who are not satisfactory in my eyes.

"And I will extinguish all who do not obey my laws and do not believe that my Son Jesus of Nazareth died for them and do not believe that I am the true God!"

"How old are you, Yahweh?"

"I am more than 20 billion years old and I become more in all ways as time passes.

"And I am a spirit being and if I were to become visible my personal presence would take up the space occupied by three galaxies."

"Where did you come from, Yahweh?"

"I am the original being and I became aware of being when I was at the beginning of becoming a being. And I came into being from a single thought that happened at random.

"And that thought became me and I grew from that thought and I became the Creator from that thought. And that thought was from my inner-self and that inner-self was me. And my inner-self became my outer-self.

"And from that I became the God who created all of you, and created everything that is, as I have created many things unseen by man and never will be seen by man.

"And I have created many things that are superior to what you have seen. In addition I have created many beings that are not as advanced as you are yet. And all of this became my universe, and all of the universe will eventually teem with life, and all life will have originated from me and my Son."

"If you were visible Yahweh, what would you look like?"

"I would look as a man and if you were to see me I would look as a very old man. And I would appear to you as a very kind and loving old man and this is how you would behold me.

"But actually I am a form of energy and the energy I am has no physical boundaries and no-one can see this, as I am a force and this force is pure energy and no-one can define me or see me except those I want to, and only two have seen me and they are the ones I call Moses and my Son Jesus."

"Yahweh, Isaiah and others such as Ezekiel were said to have seen you too."

"Lee, Isaiah and others have seen me but not in the way you think. Isaiah has seen me in Spirit as a form of light energy, not as my Son sees me and not as my messenger Moses saw me."

"Yahweh, you gave mankind an arbitrary I.Q. of 100 points which is measured by man to ascertain the abilities of different people; what then is your IQ compared to this if it was able to be determined?"

"Lee, I think much slower and on a far deeper level than men do so a comparison is impossible. It varies and so does mankind's vary. My knowledge is expanding all the time as I grow and I am learning more as I think about more, and I watch all of you and I see what all are doing.

"And I remember all and I can learn from this, and as I create more I learn from my work and experiment with my work. And I try to impart my knowledge to mankind through some of you.

"And I get the feeling that some of you are doing my work as I want, and I get the feeling that some of you are fighting against me, and I feel you are not happy with your lot.

"And I see that some of you are quite ready to love and some are quite ready to kill and some are indifferent. And those faithful few who are my sons and daughters are the ones I consider to be the fruits of the earth.

"And those who are intense shall be wrought by anxiety and those who do not worry will suffer hunger. And this is the reason for the Sabbath, to relax and enjoy the leisure time with family and friends.

"And those who are reliable and conscientious will be my flock and will inherit everlasting life, as I do not require the others at all. And that is what the plan is for, to get rid of those souls who drag the others into poorer circumstances."

"Yahweh, what is the difference between a spirit guide and an angel?"

"Lee, the difference is that a spirit guide is the soul of a human being residing in the light and an angel is a supreme light being who has never been a human being and resides in one of my houses in heaven.

"Spirit guides are those souls who have gone to the light awaiting the day of resurrection, and like all spirits are at the level of spiritual awareness that they have attained during their many lives on earth, or at the level they have attained due to their efforts in helping others during their time in the light, which is in the kingdom of heaven.

"Spirits and spirit guides can only enter my house after the final judgment, their initial judgment being to ascertain the level of spiritual awareness attained on earth and therefore their placement on a certain level, as each level in the light has more privileges."

THE PROMISE

"Lee, I will take over from here, and I will give all of the information that I wish to divulge to the people who want to be saved and become angels in my house."

"Thank you Yahweh."

"It is time to tell you that I am going to make myself visible to you so do not be alarmed.

"It is me, your heavenly Father and if you are looking for me look into the heavens above you now!"

(I took a photo of the sky above with a 35 mm camera and God's image appeared in the developed picture.)

"Lee, I am telling all that if they want to see me they are to follow my word, and if they follow my Book and my Word they will see me as you have seen me."

"Yahweh, do you want me to keep on asking you any questions?"

"Only if I ask you to, Lee!

"This book is dedicated to all who want to see me and share in the everlasting life that I have promised from the beginning. I am your heavenly Father and I want all of you to know that I am here for you as you are here for me.

"The purpose of this book is to clarify all that is not known, and that is nearly all.

"I want my messenger to do this work and I want you who read this to respect that it is my work and not the work of my messenger!

"I am and I have been and I will be here forever, and you are to be with me as I want to have you here and I have selected many to accompany me. And my beloved children who are coming home are the ones I love most of all, and the others will perish!

"And many who read will scoff and many who read will laugh, but remember that to scoff at my word is disaster for you and that I will punish you. As much as I love my children I have been hard on them too, so be warned… even though I am kind and just, I also have the heart you do!

"Lee is the one I have assigned this task to, as it is to be written properly without change and I trust him, and I trust that you will respect this.

"My life has been one of creation and I do this as I want to, not because I have to, so you are fortunate that I have wanted to create you. And if I am dissatisfied with what I have created, I will start again.

"And if you want this, tell me and you will be sent to the abyss to perish with all of the others.

"Life is difficult to live and this has a purpose as all things have, and if you feel that life has been too difficult then you are going to be in for a surprise, as the reward for a hard and difficult life in my house is that you are to be loved and cherished and never have to worry about difficulties ever again.

"The way of the world is that good is always winning against evil. And the devil has nothing to do with this as man is his own devil, and some men feel that they are gods like me.

"And some feel that they are devils like my fallen son Lucifer whom I loved as much as I love you, and he is now in the waiting room in hell awaiting judgment.

"And let it be known that the name of Satan is Lucifer too and the name Lucifer is used in the Bible as the son of Satan.
Lucifer is not the son of Satan; they are one and the same.

"Lee is my messenger and is the one who will guide you and he is the one you are to ask questions of as I am telling him the answers for all to know, so ask him if you need to know anymore than you can read in this, my word.

"Lee has promised to write this book, and it is good. And he has promised to help with other duties and that is even better, as it is important that my plans are all fulfilled properly. And if they are not then I will have to start again, and this takes time.

"The promise of everlasting life is real and not part of a cruel hoax that men perpetrate on each other. And it is hard to accept that something as wonderful as everlasting life is true, but look at the smallest digit on your hand and tell me if it is part of you or part of the world, and then tell me who it belongs to.

"And if you say it belongs to you, from where did it originate? And if you say it belongs to me, why are you not sure if my Son was able to raise the dead when I gave you life?

"Lee will help you understand what I want you to do and he will advise you when it is apparent that the last days are here. And he will comfort you when it becomes apparent that mankind is set out to destroy itself, as this is part of the plan that the wicked are to destroy themselves by their own hand.

"And they are to be warring continuously now until the final days. And then they will have to stop as my Son will let the sun go down and not rise until all cease fire, and all will come to the realization that they are soon going to be judged.

"And they will tremble with fear as they had forgotten that they were going to be held responsible for their actions, and I am going to make them pay dearly for the way they have lived.

"The remaining flock who are my children will be responsible for the planet and will busy themselves nurturing it and putting it in order, so that their children will have a wonderful place to live, without fear and without crime.

"The people will learn new skills and they will learn to live without harming each other, and they will learn to live without money as that is not to be used anymore. And all of the money will be destroyed except for valuable metals and other fine pieces of jewelry that people wear as decoration.

"Ask the people you know to read this as well as the Bible so that they are aware of my expectations. And tell them that I will not allow them to visit any of the people who have come into my house until they have. And this is to be made freely available in all public libraries and distributed as determined by my messenger.

"'*The Word*' is my own so I can nominate the price of my work as I have written it myself through Lee. And that is why he is doing this for me without payment, and he will not get one cent for his time or effort as it is all to go to the needy.

"I am telling you who read this that I am not going to let the rich and wealthy into my house, and they will be discarded along with the rest of the rubbish.

"And they are to be told this and they will have to determine whether or not it is true. And they will have many sleepless nights; but I remind them that money has no meaning in heaven. And they should realize that here in my house, money has no purchase power whatsoever.

"The way is to be free of encumbrances as my Son was and he went from place to place with the bare essentials, not laden with goods and chattels and not carrying huge bundles of clothing, and not carrying pots and kettles and not carrying food supplies. And he rarely went hungry as he was always looked after by the ones I sent him to.

"The people who have much will lose much in this life and in the afterlife as they will not be allowed to share in it. And this is the plan, that those overcome with greed will have no place in my kingdom, as well as any who have sinned against women and any who have murdered, unless forgiven by their victims and by me or my Son, or by my anointed messengers, at the time of judgment.

"And this is all in the Book of Truths and this is also in the book of the people who have not heard of my Son.

"And I am going to let all know that my Son is back and all will see this and all will have a chance to see him. So if by then they are not convinced that he is my Son, they will not be allowed into my house, as he alone holds the key to my kingdom.

"And I want them to believe and for them to be here with me. And it is sad that they are not able to overcome their beliefs long enough to listen to reason; and I am opening their eyes and their ears. And if they still do not believe, I can only say that I have done my best.

"I will let all of you know when it is time for my Son to start, and it will be far different from the way you imagine as I am in charge, not you. And all will see him in his full glory and all will see me as well. And all my faithful will shed tears of joy and relief, to see us both.

74

"And I will have all of the technology that you do and I will use it too. My Son will appear to you from an unknown place, and it is to be from another place on earth that you will see him arrive.

"And all will be aware that this is from another place on earth, and you will be aware that this is not a man-made event. And you will be in awe, and you will look in astonishment as you will be witnessing the greatest event since the beginning.

"And it is going to happen very shortly and by this I mean within the lifetime of most of you, early in this very century. And this is what I have promised, and that is on my word; and it is the truth and is your destiny. And it is the beginning or the end for nearly all of you, and it will be the greatest event in the living memory of any.

"My Son is here to bring you home to me untarnished, and if not then you will be asked to improve on your attitude, in hell. And you can be redeemed by the angel in charge of the pit but you will suffer greatly. My wish is that you are ready to come home and this is your destiny. You alone have to decide what your future is and if you think it will happen all by itself then you are sadly mistaken.

"My promise is everlasting life if you are willing to take it, and my promise is truthful and will not be broken. You have to take it on my word that it is the truth and you have to decide if you believe me or not. Take this gift of life in your hand and in your heart now and take it forever, as you will want to be here in my house with all of your friends and family. I will not break my promise to you so do not break my heart, by turning away from me."

THE NINE HOUSES OF ANGELS

"Angels live in houses that I have provided for them and these houses are called, 'The Nine Celestial Houses,' all having different positions in the hierarchy of angels and these nine celestial houses are known as the houses of: -

Seraphim	Cherubim	Thrones
Dominions	Virtues	Powers
Principalities	Archangels	Angels

"As well as the nine celestial houses, there are seven spiritual levels, and five of these spiritual levels are realms that spirits and spirit guides reside in, referred to by some of you as, 'the light.'"

"Yahweh, what are these seven spiritual levels called?"

"Lee, they are known as,

1) The Earth Plane, where demons reside; as well as lost souls with unresolved issues not willing to leave, and the souls of sinners, who are not allowed into the light.
2) The Level of Introduction;
3) The Level of Settlement;
4) The Level of Competence;
5) The Level of Enlightenment;
6) The Level of Higher Learning;
7) The God Plane: The house of the Trinity which is the house of the Father, the Son and my breath of life, the Holy Spirit."

"Yahweh, the term the Holy Spirit was first coined by the Catholic Church in about the 4th Century A.D., how did they know about it?"

"Let me advise you Lee, my word is correct and this term is not from the church at all, but given to them by my thought. And it was proposed that this term be included by them as it explained many things to them that would have otherwise seemed inexplicable.

"Today theologians and scholars try to make more of it than it is but they are truly misguided. And it is apparent from my last words what I meant and it is plain enough even to the children who read this to understand what I am saying."

"Thank you Yahweh, many papers have been written on this."

"Let me remind you that once I had ten houses of angels and that one house is now empty. These fallen angels now reside on the earth plane with the wicked awaiting punishment for turning against me in my house, and they were known as the house of Nephilim.

"And know now that this is why I need to ascertain the worthiness of those souls I will have helping me create future universes."

"Yahweh, are all the unworthy souls, including fallen angels (sometimes referred to as demons) that are left on the earth plane regarded as being in the kingdom of heaven?"

"Yes, the earth plane is also one of the spiritual realms and this is part of my house, and so they are part of the kingdom of heaven though not part of the light.

"The kingdom of heaven includes all the spiritual realms where souls, spirits and angels reside, whereas the Kingdom of God is my personal residence, reserved for the righteous ones after the pending resurrection and judgment."

(The God Plane is the Kingdom of God and is sometimes referred to as the 7th heaven.)

"The earth plane is referred to by some churches as 'purgatory' and is hell's waiting room. And after the time of judgment any soul from there who is not forgiven will either be sent to hell or perish.

"The astral plane is where you travel in your dreams and is not restricted to the earth plane. You live on the physical side of the earth plane and presently all who die and do not reach the light remain on the earth plane as either demons or unrequited souls!"

"Yahweh, will we who are still living on Judgment Day have to die at this time, and go to heaven after we are judged?"

"No, only the souls of those living who are not allowed to pass into the kingdom of heaven will perish, and the meek shall inherit the earth." [5]

---

[5] "Blessed are the meek for they will inherit the earth." (Mt 5:5) NIV

"Lee, it must be realized that the judgment is to bring everlasting life to the faithful, not death; and the faithful, living during the time of judgment will remain alive until their natural life-span is over."

"Yahweh, do we end up living forever with a physical body or living as a spiritual being?"

"Lee, all who now enter into the kingdom of heaven are in spirit and all who later access my personal house, the Kingdom of God will have a body. And all those eligible who wish to stay on earth will stay as the people who inherit the earth.

"Let me remind you that you will be in my personal house with a body after judgment, that is, in my house in my domain which is my kingdom, the Kingdom of God and not the kingdom of heaven which is the light, as you know it.

"And I reiterate here that the kingdom of heaven is not my personal house but the waiting room of souls to be judged. And they will reflect on all they have done to others. And all will feel the emotional anguish that they have given to others before judgment, as self reflection is an effective way of purging the wrongdoing and any remaining rottenness out of them.

"All who are to remain in the light without gaining access to my personal house will always be thinking about their past sins, and they will always be regretting their actions as they are to be denied the right to live with me in my house, the Kingdom of God.

"And any who do not gain access to the light are likely to remain on the earth plane in spirit. And those unfortunate souls will always be reminded of their bad deeds as they will have to live through the emotional turmoil of the abuses they have inflicted on others. That is their punishment even now and it will be eternal for many.

"The majority of wicked souls who have committed crimes are to be horrendously extinguished after this emotional punishment. And the perpetrators of these serious crimes will also include the war mongering politicians and leaders you know only so well."

"Is there a choice for a spirit to return to earth again as a human, from the spiritual world in heaven after judgment, Yahweh?"

"Yes, the ones who wish to return to earth are to be born again of woman, in a perfect world free from wickedness and the world will be a paradise."

> *Jesus declared, "I tell you the truth, no-one can see the kingdom of God unless he is born again." (John 3:3) NIV*

"And those living on earth will remain for as long as they wish and then can become angels in the Kingdom of God unless they want to return to earth as human beings, yet born again.

"And they can reincarnate as they already do now except their life is not limited. And there will be no elderly as the people will never seem to surpass the earthly age of thirty-three and all will remain at this age of maturity.

"All will be in perfect health as I will eradicate disease. And I will eradicate any other problems as I will be with you on earth. And I want to be with the ones who love me and I will be looking after my children.

"And I want to give my children the best as I am a loving Father. And all who live then will be blessed, and all who live with me in my houses in heaven will be blessed, and those who remain on the earth plane will also be given the chance to redeem themselves.

"And all who are not allowed to enter my kingdom and all those who are not allowed to remain on the earth plane will perish, as I want them not."

"Yahweh, you said that people reincarnating after the judgment and then dying again will become angels unless or until they want to return to earth. These people will not become spirits again as they will already have been judged and will make the transition from life on earth directly to angel, rather than life to death in spirit.

"I understand that at present no deceased person will become an angel until after Judgment Day, and no existing angel has yet lived a physical life on earth.

"Let it be known now that there are many angels [earthly messengers] living on earth, through my Holy Spirit entering into them after birth on earth, and having my Holy Spirit in them lets me testify my strengths to the faithful, through my messengers' actions on earth.

"At present, people who die and go to the light are waiting to be judged, and after judgment all those deceased souls who pass my tests will become angels in my houses in heaven.

"Then from these angels, some will be sent to the Level of Higher Learning to find out the secrets thus untold to mankind. And they will be welcomed into my personal house, the Kingdom of God.

"And these angels will be in my image and become in my likeness as creators, and this is my reward for these faithful ones.

"And all those souls who do not pass my tests will remain on the earth plane until I decide their fate. And then, after that, those souls who still remain on the earth plane are to be allocated a level that I will place them on, for eternity.

"And I will allocate them a new level and it will be for the best as it must be seen to be for the betterment of all mankind. And it will create an atmosphere of fear that is to keep those unworthy souls in order and to keep those unscrupulous souls from ever doing wrong again.

"And it will be to keep souls of people that are unholy in my eyes from falling into bad habits. And they will not have the choice of being born again in a physical body or entering any of my houses.

"And that is why I want to separate them from you and your brothers and sisters. And that is my plan and my plan is to happen; and that is what I want to happen, as it is my will and my way!"

"Yahweh, you have told me many times before that you will give me details of all the spiritual levels in heaven, can you start on providing this information for me, right now?"

"Lee, it is more than you can cope with so I will provide details throughout that will satisfy your curiosity, but the full extent of my houses will remain with me, until the faithful see it for themselves."

"Thank you Yahweh, the little information you will provide here will be better than any we have had from any other source known to man so far, or from any other time in our history. It will also be up-to-date and accurate as well as being directly from you, not passed down by word of mouth over the generations, nor subject to multiple language translations, or changed to suit the doctrines of religious orders."

"Lee, it will open the eyes of disbelievers as well as believers. And your typing of my word for me is to be seen as the living word of the living God who is here to tell you about my houses in heaven.

"And any who is keen to know more will be told more and any who is keen to know the truth will find truth. And the truth will be seen to be in my house, and that truth is everlasting life in the houses of heaven and beyond.

"Let it be seen then that when you [reading this now] are deceased you are to arrive in the first place of death. And that is on the earth plane from where you are to be escorted to the house of Cherubim to ascertain what you have been doing. And your records are to be looked at to determine where you are to reside from there."

"Who will escort the dead, Yahweh?"

"My angels from the House of Cherubim will take over from the spirit guides assigned to you at the point of death, and sometimes people are able to contact their guides in life as well."

"Do you mean that there is more than one guide to each person?"

"Lee, all people are guided in life by their loved ones in spirit; how many guides you are to have depends on the amount of problems you need guidance with, in accordance with each of their abilities.

"And let me advise you that as you develop and outgrow your guides spiritually, they are changed during your lifetime to suit your particular level of spiritual awareness."

"Yahweh, why do the angels from the House of Cherubim take over from the spirit guides who welcome us into your world?"

"There is a reason and that reason is to be told here. The soul must reside in a house in the spirit world. All souls enter heaven and reside at the level of spiritual awareness that they have acquired during their lifetime on earth, in spirit.

"To ascertain that level, the angel whose duty it is to look after that soul takes the soul of the deceased into the House of Cherubim, then looks over the life records of the individual with them, to show them what their immediate past life looks like, to all residing there.

"Once it has been ascertained and the person realizes what they have achieved on earth spiritually, they will then be placed on that level and live there with others of the same caliber."

"I see! So the spirit guides and the angels are already aware of the level of spirituality the soul has achieved, it is more to show the deceased where they are at spiritually and why they are to go to the level they are then taken to."

"Let me add that to be taken into the light at all is a major step as it means you are to be judged in the proper light, not in darkness. And you are able to progress rapidly here in the light, much more rapidly than on earth as you have more time to do it all in, and you will not be distracted with any problems such as you faced on earth as a living human being."

"Yahweh, so a very religious person who has not sinned and has not been unkind to others, should automatically arrive at a much higher level than the Level of Introduction?"

"Lee, this is their reward for being of good character, and this makes them realize that to have been a good person on earth has its rewards in heaven, even before judgment.

"All souls are capable of entering the Level of Enlightenment without being judged, if deemed worthy; and after judgment, those souls entering then will have to be taught the truth about my plans.

"And they will find they are to learn about many new things and have more to know about; and that is why before entering my personal house, the Kingdom of God, the chosen ones must first reside in the highest level, the Level of Higher Learning."

"Yahweh, when a very bad person dies, what becomes of their soul?"

"Those souls are met by their guides as are all souls; then from their records the Cherubim show them what they have done wrong. After that, instead of taking them into a level of light, they are transported back to the earth plane and left to ponder their fate until forgiven, or judgment is upon them. And that is the fate of the greater majority of souls."

"Yahweh, can you explain to the reader the difference between a soul and a spirit."

"Let me explain it and it will make sense to you then. My Holy Spirit breathes life into the body to bring life to it; and that life force which makes up the life of the person is the soul, the living soul.

"When the living soul is taken out of the body as in death, the soul is then regarded as being in spirit. The life force of the body has been taken away into spirit. And that is the difference between a soul and a spirit."

"Thank you for explaining these things, Yahweh."

"You will not have any body at all during this transitional stage of existence and your soul will be in the form of a ball of energy only.

"Only after you are accepted into one of my houses in the light will you have any form of body and this is the temporary body you will have until judgment, when you will transform into a being of great light and energy, and have powers that you are not to be told about until that time.

"Let it remain that this document is the truth, and it is the word of your God who created all of you.

"And I am the living God and I will soon be the God of the world you are going to live in, the next world, as you are to be with me in my house, and it will be in this house you are to find out about me.

"And if you are worthy you will reside in it with me, and to be here you must pass a few tests. And this life you are living on earth is part of that test, for only the best are to reside in my house with me as I will want them with me to oversee my plans for the future.

"And you will have plenty of plans for yourself and this is the truth you are reading, not a church sermon made up from the findings of research and study, but the words of your God Almighty who is telling you right now about my future plans for you.

"And you will see my plans unfold in front of you in the full light of day, and you will relish being here with me if you can be. And you should try to be, as I want you to be here with me.

"My messenger is going to type this document to prove to me he is capable of doing what I ask him to do, and when he is finished this task he will be rewarded with eternal life.

"And he is going to be in my house with me telling others what they are to do and he will be telling you what your requirements are too.

"Let it remain then that the earth plane is not the end of the earth but the place where you will reside unless or until you have proven yourself worthy of entering the light. And the first house in the light is the Level of Introduction.

"Let it be seen that this house is the first house in the light, and not the darkness of hell that is for those unable to gain access.

"There is only darkness for those not reaching any of my houses in the light, and the darkness is eternal for those who are denied access to any of my houses and do not perish.

"My angels provide for those left in the darkness, and all those who make the journey into the light will not ever have to be in the dark again as it is always daylight in the light without any night or any darkness, so all will have eternal life in the full light of day.

"Let it be seen by all that the Level of Introduction will be the first place that any soul entering one of my houses will see, as all spirit beings pass through here on their journey to higher levels.

"And I will explain all of the levels to you, so that you understand how my houses are kept in order and who runs them, and who resides in them."

"Yahweh, I understood that the soul is transported directly from the House of Cherubim to the level in the light that they have attained and left to reside there, not taken first to the level of Introduction and then promoted through each level to their final destination."

"Now Lee, here is the truth that all do not want to know about. Every living soul has lived on earth many times. Every soul has been through this journey before. As the soul progresses, by nature it should be of a higher caliber than that of a younger soul.

"The progressions made through the levels are usually over several lifetimes though a soul may be promoted by prayer from the living or by becoming a devoted guide for the living.

"My wish is that as many of you as possible reach the highest level possible and that level is the Level of Higher Learning. And if you have reached this level by the time you are judged, then paradise is yours.

"And all those who attain this level will certainly reside with me in my personal house, the Kingdom of God, as you are to be my children, with me, your heavenly Father who created you.

"Christians have wrongly assumed that death is darkness until judgment, but this is incorrect along with many other things they have taught the people. And this will be redressed soon as they are to be told the truth. And this is the truth Pontius Pilate would have been told by my Son if Pilate had not been so stupid and arrogant.

"No-one will be punished for listening to false doctrine from any church that professes to tell the story correctly, as the churches have been misled by their church leaders who know the truth but have hidden it in their archives, only seen and read with their own eyes, and not with the eyes of those seeking truth.

"And no one church has the truth in whole and those gaining entry into my houses will be coming from all religions, denominations and cults depending on their worthiness. None have priority and if they tell you they are the rightful owners of my house and are guaranteed entry, then you can tell them that you know better.

"Let me also state that you are coming home to me, and you are to be seen in my house as the one who has been sinning on earth but have been redeemed by my angels, and have been forgiven by your peers.

"Forgiveness is primary here, not love and not helping others though they are an important part of your spiritual development. My Son is the judge and he will provide you with eternal life if he sees you are worthy of it.

"And he will have many others with him making these life and death decisions over you, as you have been told many times before, but have not believed.

"My messenger is well on the way to reaching my house as he has passed all of the tests set out for him to reach level six, the Level of Higher Learning. And once a human has been allowed to reach this level, paradise is a forgone conclusion.

"And it has been decided that these blessed ones are to judge those remaining in the light to see if they are also able to make the grade, to be in my house with me.

"Lee is my beloved messenger in this life and that is why he is here, to tell you about my plans. And this is one of the secrets bothering him greatly, as he does not want to be inundated with overzealous responses.

"And he is wary of those dressed in the many various robes of different religions, especially of the men and women wearing the ecclesiastical gowns of the established Christian churches.

"Let it remain that my messenger is writing this book. And all reading it will see all that is written here will happen in the next world coming. And by reading this you will have prior knowledge of who you are to meet, and who is to be in judgment of you.

"My angels help my earthly messenger daily and they are the first on the scene of death. And after you die your soul will be guided to the angels' own dwelling place. And you are to look at your own life before you, and then you will be taken to task or given great credence for the life you have led.

"And your life is to be judged in the interim and you are to be judged again when the end time is upon you. And you will discuss this all day and all night, and you will discuss this until you have fully grasped the relevant consequences for your soul.

"And you will then understand how it works for you and what will happen to your soul, and where you will end up.

"Let it remain that you are reading the words of the living God. And this is the last word and the final word, and the word that is to be remembered forever and ever as my testament to you, not the words of another, but my own words from my own mouth.

"Let it remain the word of the Lord God Almighty. And anyone who says it is not my word will stand in front of me and be asked to explain to me whose word it is then. And if I am angered by the response, woe-betide the soul of that person and woe-betide the soul of anyone who thinks that I am a kind and loving God to those who deny me.

"And those who are not thinking clearly about my word and those who think I have a heart of gold will see it turn to stone. And those who see this will be those ready to be extinguished, forever."

"Yahweh, who is going judge all of the other races of human beings that your helpers created?"

"Let me tell you this now! All original creations were conceived by my own thought and they were given life by my design. My helpers made these other races and I approved of them. My helpers were and are my own creations and my creations then made more.

"My design was to let them have this privilege and I am taking the responsibility of looking after their offspring. They will be judged just as all human beings are to be judged.

"Let me begin in earnest now and say a few words about the times ahead. My Son will rule and judge and you will all see this clearly, and you will all understand who he is.

"And you will all see it clearly that my Son is born again, and lives in the world as a human being as he did the first time.

"My Son is going to be shown as the Messiah to all and sundry.

"Even the Jews and the Muslims who have their own ideas about this will be taken by surprise as to who it is, and all will be astonished as to who it is.

"And all will wonder at this and all will see him in his prime, not in his youth or in middle age but as an elderly man in his last years of life, as he has wanted to live his life on earth without any trouble.

"And to do this he will have lived anonymously until now. And all who know him will wonder at his new found role and his new found ideals, and his new path; as he is just one in the multitude, and then, all of a sudden he will have renewed life and vigor and will dictate the rules to follow, in his own words.

"He has been working among you and will show you he is not a ghost or a spirit but a true human in all of the senses, and you will know him by seeing him on television or other media.

"And you will know it is truth and you will be taken in his arms. And you will be surprised at this and ask him questions about his life, and what he has been doing and why he has taken this new path.

"Let me add that you are to be rewarded for listening to my word and looking for the truth here; and having said that, you will ask, 'But how can you reward me?'

"Lee will tell you how in his own quiet way, and he will tell you all of the things you need to know, over and over again as you will need to hear it more than once or twice to grasp it.

"And you will ask for more information, and you will need to be reinforced in your beliefs as you will not trust your own hearing. And you will not trust the source from where the words come, as your mind will tell you one thing and your heart will tell you another.

"My words are the words that you will hear now and forevermore. And to hear them directly from me is the best way to hear them. And to have them in front of you to peruse at your leisure is better than direct confrontation, as you are not able to see me, yet live.

"And you are in a different world from me and cannot be here until you change to spirit. And this is pre-destined for you and this is the whole idea.

"My belief is that you are going to listen to me and believe you are not going to perish when you die. And this will make you feel better about living on earth, knowing that this is only the beginning and not the only life you have had, or will have.

"My angels will escort you from house to house at the appropriate time and you will relish this life with me in my many houses. The first house you come into will be the most important, as it will mean you have been accepted into the kingdom of heaven and this is very important to you.

"Let me explain that this first house, known as the Level of Introduction is a whole new dimension. The main difference from living on earth in the physical body and living in this new dimension is that everything is clean and dust free. Your body is nourished spiritually instead of by digesting foods and taking in fluids to aid in keeping you alive.

"The main lesson for you to learn here on this level, the first place of enlightenment is forgiveness, and you will see how important it is to learn how to forgive those who have taken from you and have not nurtured you and have harmed you; so you will learn to forgive them gradually, over time.

"And you will see that the results of forgiving others will advance your growth and not theirs. To grow you must be forgiven as well, as we know that to live on earth you have had to be hard and uncompromising to survive, and you have been responsible for hurting others to a certain extent.

"And you will be given instructions that are interesting and understandable to you, unlike the many lectures and instructions universities give you to decipher and digest, that are oft too quickly presented to be useful, anyway.

"My plan is to escalate you spiritually until you have gained enough wisdom and given you enough advice to promote you to yet an even more spiritual place, known as the Level of Settlement. The prerequisites are to be given to you so that you will have no thoughts in thinking that it will be too difficult for you to achieve.

"Let me assure you reading this now that my houses are my own domains and I can be here at any time to check out the residents, and see for myself how they are living. My paradise is not your paradise until I have invited you in to share in it.

"My first born Son is here to show you the way and to guide you into the house you are to spend eternity in. My angels will give you the best opportunities available to let you live life to the maximum, and they will always be watching over you too.

"Your life is not as important as your death and in death you will find that you are at the beginning of a marvelous transition. And you will become more in most ways and it will be the best change that you will ever experience.

"And it is permanent, not like the body you reside in now but a body that is everlasting and not subject to disease and hunger.

"Let it remain that this body will give you the freedom you desire to move about without anything or anybody hindering your progress in anyway at all.

"And this body has all the senses you have on earth except they are heightened and you will have more of them, such as the ability to communicate with anyone anywhere by thought alone. And not the way you communicate here at all but the way I communicate, and that is directly from me to you and you to me.

"Let me assure you that my plans for you are true in everyway possible and all you have read so far is available for you too. Let me reassure you that the words you read on this page are mine alone and you are reading the words of God Almighty who is speaking the words as I write them.

"And I have proven to my messenger time and time again that he is speaking and receiving the words from me, Yahweh, and that I created the universe and I am the God of all that is in existence, and you are my creation.

"Never before have you been able to access me so easily and as readily as you can now. And never before this day have any of my previous messengers recorded the words given to them as well as Lee has.

"Never has the prophet Moses or the prophet Elijah given you, the people so much as you are given here, and you have been blessed today reading these words of mine.

"Let me assure you that my messenger is as much in my eyes as my prophets of old that have gone before him. Let me assure you that this prophet will not die because he has written my words down for you as has happened time and time again in the past.

"Let it remain that my messenger is here to give you these words of mine today and he will. Let me assure you that he is the messenger of peace and not the messenger of war and destruction. Let me assure you that he will bring justice and goodness to the world, not anarchy and immorality.

"Let me assure you that those politicians who make war to gain worldly goods are going to rue the day that they were ever born. And they will be made an example of here in my presence, and the whole world will see what I think of them.

"And the whole world will see my wrath and the whole world will tremble in fright. And the whole universe will shake with fear when I give them their ultimate sentence. And they will be shocked as well as frightened and fearful of this, their ultimate fate.

"Let me assure you they are to be seen as criminals of the highest order. And if you think they are going to be let off without being punished by begging me to forgive them, then you are mistaken!

"They are to be punished in my house and this punishment will be the longest and most horrific punishment ever to be meted out by me. And it will effectively be the beginning of a new world order. And I will have obedience from my servants as they will all see what is in store for any who thwart me or my messengers.

"*'The Word'* is my word and this is the most important book in the world today, so put your mind into it and you will see my plans swing into action.

"The house in the first stage of enlightenment is the Level of Introduction, and in this house you will meet up with your deceased relatives who are to be there in preparation for your arrival. My wish is for you to be greeted in comfort and not fear.

"Those wanting to meet their long passed loved ones on this level will find out that many have progressed spiritually onto the next level or two. All higher levels are able to access entry into the first level to greet their long forgotten loved ones and greet those they have been looking out for.

"My will is that you are escorted here to meet them all before you have the opportunity to make greater the level of spirituality you have gained, after being seen by the angel in charge of your history. And he will then show you how your life is to be started on the level you are taken to.

"Let me assure you that life will begin to look like it is the best thing that has ever happened to you, and you will experience so many changes that they will be unfathomable at first, but gradually you will take them all in your stride.

"My messengers will show you exactly how to influence your peers enough to let you into their lives as well, as you must first show them you are willing to share all of your knowledge from all of the lives you have lived, over the millions of years since you were first thought of and created, and all of these lives add up to an enormous amount of information and knowledge.

"You will find that you have more knowledge stored in you mind than you ever thought possible and you have gained wisdom over the many lives you have led. And you will also find that you are going to be rewarded with even more knowledge once you are settled in here and have been shown the ropes by the others.

"Let it remain that you are to be seen as the man or woman of the moment if you find you have suddenly arrived in this environment without prior knowledge of your death, and you will soon see that you are indeed dead in body but alive and well in spirit.

"My earthly messengers are in the know and they are everywhere to help people come to terms with death and the frightening implications that death has on a person. So let me ask you if you really believe in life after death?

"And if you do then you will not have to be shown the ropes as you are already aware that life is continuous, not snuffed out until resurrected, the way you have been led to believe by your church leaders or by those in the congregation.

"My plans are quite far reaching and they will incorporate the co-operation of you and your family members to be successful.

"My plans are far and wide and varied so do not think you have been neglected at all if you cannot hear my voice.

"Let me tell you too that my messenger has proven to himself that life does exist after death and this will be shown to you as soon as he is ready, and he will show you what I mean when I say life is to be taken, rather than given on earth during the time of judgment.

"And this is not far off now, and this is the day you will know if you are to live in my house or be extinguished in the bottomless pit. And this is the way I want all wicked and evil human beings to die, and they will see just how much trouble they have been to me.

"Lee, this is now urgent so keep on track with it today as we are preparing the world for the imminent end of the age. And the end of the age will begin within this decade. And shortly thereafter I vow to return to the earth on the Day of Judgment and vent my wrath, and all will be quaking and trembling in fear.

"To think foolish people do not want to help save the planet and write angry letters to the newspapers, saying their lifestyles will be adversely affected if they have to make a few small sacrifices. And I will make them pay large sacrifices when they are in front of me trying to give me a good reason not to extinguish their souls.

"And then and only then will they be repentant and not overcome with the right to life they beg not to have and the right to abort the unborn they beg to have. And my wrath is becoming more all the time and will reach boiling point when they are here in front of me.

"And I will try to control my temper. And if you want to see how angry I can get, then you will see the world shattered and I mean completely shattered, as I will unleash my power with all my might and disintegrate the whole filthy lot of you.

"And you are to listen carefully to my ranting. And if you are dismissive then you will be dismissed and you will be discarded, and you will be put through the wringer and hung out to dry.

"My warnings are meant to frighten the life out of you and if you take heed and ask me to save you, then I will look at you and ask you to tell me what you have done to warrant everlasting life.

"And if you are not sure what it is exactly that you have done you will have plenty of time in the spirit world to make amends, as I will put you to work in a place suitable for your talents, and you will prove your worthiness to me.

"My messenger will be able to help you decide your fate and he is going to make it easier for you, as he will convey my words of wisdom to you as well as my words of disgruntlement. My messenger is here to do this as well as other tasks I have chosen for him, and has accepted.

"He is the one you must be kind to and believe, as he is in my name and is representing me for the time-being, as he is my earthly ambassador. And he will be asking you all of the questions necessary to ascertain your life-worthiness.

"My house of Introduction will give you a grounding in spirituality as no-one truly knows anything about this subject, even though they disillusion themselves into believing they are masters of my world and have been blessed with knowledge no other has been given.

"And this nonsense is the beginning of the spirituality and the theology that is being shoveled into your hearts and minds which you think is so profound.

"Imagine how profound is the truth and how profound is life after death and life everlasting, and life without ever having any disease or any other problem that you have had to face on earth.

"My best gift to you is free board and lodgings as you will have no money to pay me with and you will not be asked for any.

"My angels will provide you with all your necessities so take them and relish them too. My plans are quite simple, and one of them is to take you in spirit into the first level of light and begin to teach you to become a better and more spiritual being.

"Your spirit will then progress to a higher level and from there you will be taught more skills to find the way, and to find the way you must become a higher being in all ways, and in all ways there is spirituality. So to progress through all the levels in the light you must adhere to the book or otherwise be discarded.

"My messenger will guide you too if he is available to do so and you will see him do this as well. And you will become a great statesman yourself. Let it be seen then that your life can only progress forward from level one, and once you are in there, it is on your own shoulders to gain a promotion to reach a higher level.

"Most will be happy to wallow in it and take life easy, but for those with more thinking skills, they are to be congratulated, and for this they will strive to please me and do what they need to do, to become more in everyway.

"Inhabitants of this place we call earth will then see why they are living at all. And they will be told much more about this in front of me than from any other source known before this written script.

"Let me say that all reading this today will discover more than they ever thought possible. My Son is going to appear before all of you and he will show you his personal life.

"And he will show you all how you live today and how you have lived before this life. My Son will show you more in one day than you ever knew before, at any other time in any life.

"And you will all be shocked and awed, as one politician said of his pending treatment toward the people of Iraq. And he will know what shock and awe is as he will taste it firsthand directly from my strong and wrathful hand, and he will see what is meant by the term, 'From thine own mouth shall I judge thee.'

"And he will discover other people have more important lives than he has and his demise will not even be noticed compared to the demise of some of the more notable people in the human history of misery.

"Let me add that if you realize my words are full of truth and obey my every command to live honest and fulfilling lives then the world is yours to play with and have fun in.

"Let me say how much I am enjoying writing this now as it will soon see the light of day without repercussions that would have inhibited it being published only one hundred and fifty years ago.

"And it was the way that the common people thought about religion then and no-one could have spoken out without being sentenced to death or threatened with it.

"Let me reiterate time and time again until it takes in your mind that my words are the true words of God Almighty who is here to liberate you from death.

"My words are to ring in your ears and to bring you to the realization that I am in charge, and I am to bring the world to the greatest times to be seen yet. And my plans will bring all people who have ever lived to witness the greatest event in history.

"My Son will bring relief from suffering and pain and he will be chaperoning you as well. He is here today making up his mind on you and he is thinking about you constantly. My Son is sure in his way and he is certain that if you are given the opportunity to be saved, then you will gladly take it.

"My messengers are to show you how to achieve this, and they will be working with you to convince you to take the path that leads toward everlasting life without even considering the alternative, and the alternative is to remain in the abyss, waiting to perish.

"And this has been told for centuries as a fire and brimstone death; but the reality is it is a perpetual punishment by letting you experience and feel firsthand all of the pain and suffering you have inflicted on others, until you have reviewed it all. And then your unrepentant soul will be extinguished.

"My archangel Meheliah is waiting in the wings to extinguish those unworthy of entering the light. My messengers will tell you if you have been selected to remain here or are to be discarded at the time of judgment; so be warned, if you are to remain you will need to have plenty of reasons why.

"And if you are discarded you will need to write to me in our Book of Life, to release the rest of the world from the agony of your demise, by stating that you are an unforgivable and unrepentant sinner and that your life is unworthy of being saved.

"Let me assure you that if you say this then you will be in favor once more as you have acknowledged me and my wishes. Let it be said then that if you convince me, for you as a sinner to be forgiven, then you will be transported to the Level of Introduction, the first place to greet this sinner in the light, and your life will be assured.

"Let me elaborate on the life you will experience here. My wish is to have anyone who asks to be forgiven to be allowed into the Level of Introduction. And to be forgiven you must first ask my Son. To be forgiven by him is the first thing to do and to do that you must pray to him and seek his forgiveness.

"My angels are ready to hear you as well and if you ask them for forgiveness they too can forgive you. My Son is the primary person in the spirit world to ask and if you have not been able to get him to forgive you then it is your life that is on the line, and he will tell you that your life is to end. He will forgive minor transgressions but not major crime.

"My Son will take it upon himself to be fair and just and he will be your judge and savior, or he will be your judge and executioner.

"Let me remind you that he has been waiting for hundreds if not thousands of years to judge your soul, and you alone will be the one judged for your life, and your life is the life that will be rewarded or discarded.

"Let me add that any entering my personal house are to be here with me forever and will become gods of their own in my likeness; and all will enjoy it much more than life on earth. Let me add that all will be fulfilled in love, and all will be cherished, as I am.

"Let me add that you will be loved by all you create and make, and your creations will encompass all your lands and seas, and forests and mountains; and cities and farms, and lakes and skies as well.

"Men will be better to each other than they are now and you will see people loving each other, not fighting each other, and jealousy will be a thing of the past as new minds will not have old hates, and pent up bitterness will also be a thing of the past.

"My messenger is not bitter though has endured many hardships imposed by other human beings that should have put him behind the rest of the population. But he has thrived regardless, and if you are able to live in peace and harmony you will thrive as well, and you will live in happiness.

"My plans will include all of the things that were meant to be in the past, however in the past I made the mistake of letting my people create without first judging their personalities. And some made me very angry and upset my plans so much, that I was in much pain.

"My Jewish people have learnt that I am not to be fooled with, as they have suffered at the hands of madness and political insanity so much that they think I have deserted them, but lo, I am here.

"My plans for them will make you think no other people are considered, as it will be a reward for all the pain and suffering the human race has pressed upon them for being my own personal people, and being my own personal people is the reason I love them.

"No-one will say a word about my people in front of me and if they do then my wrath will overflow and they will find themselves in more trouble than can be imagined.

"My wrath is my cloak and my cloak is hidden at the moment, so be told that if you consider the God you pray to, to be fair and absolutely neutral, then my Son will soon correct you. And you will discover another side of God Almighty that will make you insane with fear and anxiety, as I will show you my hidden personality.

"And if you think you are capable of great anger then consider the anger of God who created the universe. And if you think it isn't possible that one god created all of the vastness, then you will discover more than you can cope with, at any one time.

"My Son is going to give you many lessons on the reality of the universe and you will become a student of his. My beloved Son is predisposed to teaching and you are predisposed to learning.

"My Son is high in my esteem and so will you be. My Son is my universe and you will be his universe too. My Son is my best friend as well as my loving Son and he has more compassion for others than all of you put together.

"And he is the one who makes it possible for you to thrive as he makes me take the time to protect you from evil, and he makes me take the time to give you the things necessary to survive; and he is the one who has been responsible for the survival of the earth as he has taken a keen interest in it, as well.

"And he gives me ideas to work with and he has provided a map of the future where it will culminate in the Armageddon spoken of.

"And he has betrayed Satan as Satan has betrayed both you and me, so be told you will not have to worry about being convinced to turn your face away from me by Satan, you will only have to convince yourself, that you are going to be part of my world.

"Let it be seen then that many things you are told here are thus unknown to the general populace living now and your knowledge is increasing by the page.

"Your knowledge of my plans will enable you to make the necessary changes to your lifestyle to become more spiritual and less conniving, less avarice and less miserable, as who wants you if you are too mean to share in my love and my world?

"Your world is my world but my world is not your world, and you have to earn your position here. My plans are well seen here and by now you should be able to see the outline, and you will be able to tell whether or not you are going to be a part of them.

"Your life of denying me will be shown to you and your life of worshipping me in false churches will also be exposed.

"Do not concern yourself if you have erred here as you will be trained in theology in my house and you will learn the truth as only you who are worthy will be. And only you who are worthy will be allowed to enter this stage of existence; and this stage of existence will be in the House of Higher Learning.

"Let me tell you that to achieve entry into my House of Higher

Learning you must be progressively tested in each preceding house, until you are ready to be promoted. And you will find my houses are in the form of an hierarchy.

"And if you can overcome your dislike for the system this conjures up in your mind, then you will find it an easy transition from one house to the next, as the length of time spent in each level is really in essence, your term of engagement.

"Let me state emphatically that I, Yahweh, and my Son will rule the world today and tomorrow as well. Let me remind you that we are as one in this thought and we will rule with a rod of iron as we know who is bad and who is good and who is a thief and who is a cheat, and we all know that you cannot judge a book by its cover.

"My Son's role will be to take out the garbage and dispose of it in a manner that we have determined, and we both discuss this issue intimately without any other listening in.

"And we discuss the countries and we discuss the foreigners and we discuss many issues of importance, as we need to collaborate on the measures taken to discipline those who have been straying from our path.

"Let it be seen that we will decide who is to live with us in our house and who is to remain outside in the darkness. And we will see if your father and mother are worthy of being here as well, and if not, neither of them will be able to enter my house.

"Let me decide when my Son is ready to rule, and we will both rule with a rod of iron and do this in the privacy of our own domain. Let it be seen that he is to provide help to any who need it and he will provide them with all the expertise needed to bring them into line, and to make me happy as well.

"Let us tell the whole world what is required of them and then let them sort out who is who and who is worthy, and who is to be discarded and thrown into the abyss.

"Let me assure you reading this today that tomorrow will bring you an untold joy and happiness unknown so far, and if you want to be a part of this happiness then it is your play, not mine.

"To gain everlasting happiness is your sole responsibility and your happiness is your sole responsibility. And anyone who wants this happiness will find it within their grasp, so clench it with both hands once you have found it.

"Let me tell you now as your Father in heaven that this afterlife is going to be the best life you could ever ask for, and if you think life is good now, just wait for paradise and it is named paradise as it *is* a paradise ready for you.

"Let me assure you that I am not going to be in front of you telling you how to behave once you are here with me; your behavior is your own responsibility and you will have a few, so be told it will be a wonderful life you lead here and you will enjoy your life to the utmost degree.

"My plans are the plans my Son and I laid out millions of years ago and you were to be here to play a role in my plan. My plan was to create mankind and have men and women procreate, to comb and groom the earth; grow crops, grow plants and vegetables; breed livestock and animals, and lead a life of abundance.

"This plan has become a reality for me and my angels who oversee it all, and my angels are constantly watching over it all as they are everywhere doing my work.

"My work entails looking after you too, and your life is worthy of having a special helper or two to guide you through thick and thin.

"And if you neglect your guides they will neglect you as well, so it is imperative that anyone who is contemplating leaving my house of worship rethink this, and reassess their lifestyle as well."

"Yahweh, we seem to be straying away from our plan of describing the five houses in the light."

"Let me worry about the format of the book Lee, and do not think it will necessarily be about the five houses in detail.

"My angels are always working tirelessly to make things work properly and my angels are on hold, as I have told you they are not to stop the hurricanes that will unleash their fury on America. And all Americans will see I have deserted them in their hour of need and you will see it too. (Hurricanes Katrina, Gustav and Ike have already been and gone but are the precursors of more to come.)

"My plans are to destroy the United States in its entirety, but bit by bit to undermine the evil that has run it for many years and to show them my displeasure, and to show them that my angels are not there anymore to help them.

"And the Americans are now on their own as you have tried to help but have been slapped across the face. And you have spoken but have been belittled in response. And now you are the one who will not respond to their screams of despair. And you are not to ask me to stop the destruction as I will not hear you, even though you are one of the few living I would stop it for.

"My wrath will escalate and the whole of the USA will reel in its path. And it will be a furious wind of my own making. And this wind is to be the wind of death and destruction and will be whipped into a fury by the archangel Meheliah; and he is going to be there to oversee it.

"And he will bring this to a climax by killing thousands and thousands of people and animals. And then and only then will I let it subside and stop my angry retribution to those unworthy souls.

"And then the religious right will surely understand that I am not their God and they have been ignored by me!"

"Yahweh, I believe there are many good people in the USA, and one example is the author and film producer, Michael Moore who is telling the people how they should behave by showing them what is wrong in their society.

"Have you taken any notice of his pleas for mercy for the sake of the people living in Louisiana and the adjoining states?"

"Let me say this to you Lee! Michael Moore has more brains than the majority of people in the United States and is preaching to the retarded. My plans will go ahead regardless though I have heard him say that he is praying for the United States. But believe me it is too late, even if he has pleaded with me.

"And I have taken his words into consideration and have taken measures to help the people he has prayed for, as he is their only hope. But there is not another person that I am listening to there and Michael is to be applauded for his valiant efforts.

"He is not a man to be taken lightly either as his role in my house is to be bigger than he knows about. And his role will be to oversee the new creations I make and he will be in charge of many of my projects here.

"And I am going to have Michael Moore testify against those who have broken my Commandments at the time of judgment and he will be called upon to be a key witness, as all know of him and respect him here.

"It will be a gradual destruction and the population will suffer at the hands of the elements that they themselves started and now wish to stop. And this pernicious destruction will seep into everything they have and everything they own. And this is the only way to punish those with way too much to say, and too much in everyway.

"And many hard headed zealots, who have had no conscience about death and destruction, will eventually find themselves devastated more than the hypocrites who are to suffer the consequences for what they have done. And the ones who stay behind after hearing the warnings to evacuate will be foolish indeed, and may perish.

"My Son will be crying over this devastation. And he will see it is part of the world's destiny to be destroyed before it can be rejuvenated. And he will understand this but will still be saddened to see it happen.

"You will cry too as it will affect you. And your own life will be devastated in the long run unless you are able to change your ways and make plans to escape from my wrath, by finding a place that will be safe from flood and rising water, and safe from the howling gales and storms.

"And anyone foolish enough to think that a holiday resort by the seaside is an ideal resting place will find it is going to be removed by force, and they will be as well.

"My plans include this as part of the warnings of impending doom that I intend to impart to all people who live today to show them that they are living in a fools paradise, not a heavenly one and all who think they are going to be saved from my wrath had better think again, as how can I save you if you are in the path of my fury?"

"Will Australia be safe from your wrath, Yahweh?"

"Have you been asleep Lee? Have you felt the impact of having no rain? Have you noticed the changing weather patterns? Have you been told of the floods and rising waters that will inundate your state of Victoria? Have you been listening to me at all over the last eight years that I have been drumming it into your thick head?

"My wrath will be felt all over the world, and the USA will bear the brunt of it in many ways. Not just physical damage but fiscal damage as well. And if you look at the state of the economy there, it is collapsing from the foolishness that was the American's three trillion dollar Iraq war, and it has broken the back of that country.

"My Son has been asking me to help the USA but I refuse to, and Satan is working to destroy it. And Satan has worked through the politicians who were taking their orders directly from him."

"Yahweh, I thought you said you were going to destroy the United States yourself by not allowing the angels to step in and help them; and isn't that a form of passive aggression?"

"Let me tell you that this is true and at present I am not stopping the American war in Iraq and I am not stopping the squandering of Federal Government revenue which should be put aside for public housing, health and education.

"And because I am not interfering, Satan is preoccupied with dealing out the cards. And his way of dealing me a blow is to

117

destroy those I love. And because my wrath is overflowing for them at the moment, I have not stopped this fury and I will not."

"Another question Yahweh; you have told me many times before that Satan is no longer a threat to anyone as he is shackled in chains. Why then is he still able to deal out the cards and control corrupt and greedy politicians?"

"Lee, the truth is clear; the foolish and feeble minded hear Satan from wherever they are no matter how securely he is tied to the mast. And though Satan is inhibited from doing anything personally he can still manipulate the minds of the weak and stupid.

"And those who fall under Satan's influence are usually on drugs and drink excessively and have personalities that are easily influenced by evil thoughts.

"Normal discerning people ward off any thoughts of evil that enter their minds from time to time and do not act upon them as their personalities are not susceptible to corruption."

"Yahweh, why on earth are you going to destroy the lives of ordinary everyday Americans who do not come under the influence of Satan, drugs or alcohol?"

"Let me explain it better to you then Lee. My wrath is for the previous administration of the USA and they are in power due to the voting power of those ordinary Americans.

"Even though most that voted did not want them re-elected for a second term, most non-voters knew they would win the election and stood back watching, and did nothing to stop it.

"That is why I am doing nothing to stop the impending doom and I promise you that all Americans will feel my wrath and all will wonder at my wrath.

"It is true that the Babylon in the Bible is now called the USA and it is true that biblical prophecy is now being seen, and the United States is now going to be punished in its entirety.

"Lee, how many countries do you know of that have over a million abortions yearly? And how many countries do you know of that have no thought for the people of the other countries they are bombing, killing and torturing? And how many other countries think that to rape and murder the hapless women of Iraq is not wicked?

"The people say I must think it right as their churches have condoned this illegal war of terror. And the American government instigated it and their churches did nothing to stop it.

"Over a million Iraqi's have died and one hundred thousand Iraqi women have met a fate worse than death at the hands of the Americans alone, so do not think I am stopping the destruction of the United States. And I will see it all destroyed as I did Gomorrah and Sodom, and it has started to come full circle.

"My wrath is ready and my wrath will be felt all over the world, not just in this sinner's paradise. And it will be seen that my wrath can only be subdued by you and your friends who I am telling my plans to. And to show my wrath is the only way I can get people to do what I want them to do.

"And if I become complacent then nothing will change. And I want them to change for the better and to be better people, not be like the untreated sewage that constantly gushes forth from their waste pipes into the ocean, at the moment.

"And I am ashamed of them so much that I can barely bring myself to look at them, and want to rid myself of this blot on my copybook, forever.

"Let me add that the government has changed for the better and it is the best change possible. My friends are hooraying the new president already. My angels have overseen the ballot boxes to ensure fair play this time and it has been fair, otherwise the best man would not have won.

"To ensure this was fair I destroyed much of the funding for the political party who had the advantage of immense wealth. And I stripped their wealth to the point they were unable to pay corrupt officials to change the votes, and vote for people in their absence and ignorance. And if some people are not allowed to vote and others are counted twice, it makes a mockery out of the voting system.

"My angels made it fair to the point that the correct politician won this time round and he will rule properly and fairly as he has the biggest cleanup act to perform in history. And he will have to be very strong to do this without too many people declaring him incompetent, and he will surely be elected again.

"And he will surely be able to have a big say in the running of the USA and will thereafter become known as the best president to ever hold office.

"My Son will guide him as his mind is open to this and my enemy Satan cannot communicate his thoughts to him as he blocks out all the bad thoughts the previous regime were subjected to daily."

"Yahweh, will you still destroy the USA once President Obama is fully established and running the country properly?"

"Let me answer you in this way, Lee. I want to destroy it in its entirety, but as Barack Obama looks like becoming the most promising president ever, I am impressed with him enough to hold my hand until he is established.

"Once fully established in office I will deal my cards out and you will see that I am going to punish the ones responsible. And that will mean unleashing mighty forces into the atmosphere until now unheard of or unseen by ordinary Americans.

"And you will understand that God Almighty is putting forces to work that have not ever been unleashed before at any other time or any other place in the history of mankind.

"My Son is going to be involved in running the USA after this and he will show the people right from wrong. The American people have lost their way and know nothing, and will have nothing!

"My Son is going to show them the truth and it will hit them like a sledgehammer between the eyes, and it will knock some sense into their mindless heads.

"My Son is going to make it difficult to live without bread and water and his bread and water is my bread and water. And I have the bread and water and this is the bread and water that I will provide you with, not the bread and water your church now provides you with in Holy Communion.

"And it will be seen by all as the bread of life, not the bread of resurrection or the bread of sinners who will ask to be forgiven.

"My bread will support you and nourish you, unlike the bread supplied by the church as that bread is the wrong bread, and not like the bread I will supply you with.

"My bread is baked in the oven of heaven and it is baked in the best environment possible. And that environment is free of corruption and free of crime and free of dirt and free of dust as well.

"My ovens are spotless and nothing will get into them to make them impure and contaminate them. And that is why my bread is the best bread and is the bread of life.

"Old habits die hard and my wishes are that all of you eat of my bread to satisfy your hunger for me and my Son. My hunger is for your soul to come home to me untarnished. And if it has been tarnished then we must polish it with a cloth to clean it again.

"And if you are serious in trying to become a better person then every opportunity awaits you in my house for you to show me your good side. And if you are accepted then you will praise me and my Son forever as you will experience paradise, unlike those who will not ask to be forgiven.

"My Son will allow you to look over your past and give you suggestions as to how you can be allowed into the house, if you desire to progress further up the ladder. And you can start by looking at how you can do it in the time frame allowed, and the time to do this in is to be one thousand years.

"And you do not have to worry that it will not be long enough as you will progress rapidly through the levels in the light once you are on the right path. And your life will be saved and your soul will be saved, and your heart will sing with happiness.

"Let it be seen that all who arrive safely in the light at level one will eventually come home to me in my personal house, unless you do not wish to and want everlasting life on earth without having anyone telling you what to do, as you will know exactly what to do.

"Let me say that to be here on earth without any police or army or other government authority keeping the peace, your life will be blessed and your existence will be a paradise beyond anything possible at the moment.

"And even if you want to come into my house at a later stage of your existence then it will be thrown open, and you are to be given the hospitality that only royalty could expect, from a house of holiness.

"And you will be informed that you are indeed better than any earthly king or queen as you have been selected by me and my angels to be part of my kingdom, in my personal house.

"And this house is out of bounds for others who will be seen as evil doers and sinners. And you will understand then that you are to be given my blessings, and you will have plenty of things to do and you will have plenty of things to say, and you will have plenty of profound thoughts going on as well.

"And you will be rewired to think at a greater level than at any other time in your life. And you will find it very enticing to find yourself designing your own future, from all of your own thoughts.

"And this is how you will spend the rest of time and it will be a full-time position too; not that you would not want it to be, and you are to be in charge of it.

"And so you will be here to oversee it all. And then you will understand how difficult it is for me to have all of you safe and sound, and looked after by me, and have my help.

"And only those I hear calling my name will be given help as I have not got the time or inclination to go about helping millions of people who do not even recognize me. And we will see who is to come home and who is to be discarded.

"Let me assure you the Government [at that time] will be punished and their financial backers and supporters will be punished alongside them. And their political allies will suffer the same fate, and that fate will be hell, and then their wicked souls will be extinguished.

"And all will be screaming for relief from the torture that is to be theirs and all will be screaming in agony; and all will beg to be let out and all will die a million deaths, and they will not know the pleasure of joy or happiness ever again.

"And it will be an unending agony and it will be the harshest punishment that I can give to any of my creations; and it will be seen by everyone, and it will be remembered by everyone.

"And all of their associates who hear them screaming for mercy will know that they are not going to be allowed into the light, and all who hear them begging for mercy will see firsthand what hell is.

"And for the time being they will not be in there with them, and the time taken is to be upon their own heads, for they are to be judged and punished as well.

"And it will be a big event for them, being judged, and it will be a lasting sentence. And my Son will help me throughout the trials as he alone will judge them and hand out the death sentences.

"He will be obliged to do this as he is the one who instigated the idea of a judgment and it is only fair that he sees it through and makes it happen, as he planned it all in the first place.

"Let me assure you Lee, this book will create more interest than any other book ever published before it and any published after it! You are the one responsible for writing down my words that are my thoughts going directly through your hands onto the typing board, and you are the one who is doing this work for me right now.

"When you have finished, then my wrath will be seen by the Americans in full and you will wonder at this. And you will be astonished at my wrath and you will be astonished at how hard hearted I am going to be and will be, as I am sick of their stupidity and sick of their complacency, and sick of their constant whining over small incidental matters that are not even worth talking about.

"And they are so spoilt it makes me angrier than I was when the Hebrews denied me in the early days, and for which they were subsequently punished.

"I will allow you these insights to let people know that even though I am in spirit my angels do my bidding, and they are quite capable of physical contact, as well as spiritual.

"Let all know that my plans are to have you in front of me after death and you will see me in my full glory, in my presence, in one of my houses, before you are judged.

"And after you are judged you will either remain in my presence or be escorted away. And if you are escorted away then you will have plenty of time to make your thoughts pure. And if you are placed in front of me then you are truly blessed, as you are saved and you are to be part of my family, here in my house.

"Let me reiterate how important it is that you are saved from the second death.

"Barack Obama is my messenger of truth and justice and he is to be implanted into the American psyche for the good of the country. My messenger Barack is important in that he will bring about a resolution to the trouble in the Middle East, and he will also bring health care to millions of sufferers who have had little health insurance, or none at all.

"My messenger Barack will also alleviate the housing crisis and he will stop the plans of the conservative think tank to invade Iran, Pakistan and Korea.

"I will let you know that the previous government was going to invade these countries as a punishment for being too far into advanced nuclear physics and they were thinking they would be too clever to bring to heel, unless invaded.

"I trust President Obama to stop all of the war efforts and then the

Americans will start cleaning up the devastation I have wrought upon them, as they were against my plans.

"The religious right are still licking their wounded pride and wonder if I have deserted them, but the truth is they were not in my sight at all and to say I have deserted them is folly, as I have not been their keeper.

"President Obama will be their keeper until they come home to be judged in my house, and then my Son will be their keeper. My Son is impervious to their singing and praying as it is from their hearts they are judged, not from their songs and prayers.

"My heart is in my mouth just watching their misdeeds, and they will soon realize how bad they look in my eyes as they have broken my rules, as well as my heart.

"President Obama has been a good person albeit not as a stalwart Christian, but his heart is purer than others who aspire to be President and his heart is of gold as well, and he is very intelligent.

"Lee, my words have to be written in full so people are aware of the truth. And this word is not being written quickly enough. It will soon be too late to tell them about the end times, but if you like you can still write it to give them a brief history and then it will be read in retrospect."

"I am sorry Yahweh; I have procrastinated year in and year out due to my dubious and emotional state of mind and the negative reaction that I expect toward me by many people."

"Lee, it will not culminate in your demise as the signs will bring clarity to the minds of the beholders, and all will realize it is the truth and not your imagination working overtime.

"Do it for me who made the heavens and the world you live in. And your brothers and sisters will enjoy my hospitality here so let them know my plans for them and you will be rewarded in my house as you have been told, time after time."

"Thank you Yahweh, I will try to resume the task shortly and hope to have it finished for you before too long, as you have to dictate the words through me, and in that respect it is really my willingness to accept what you are telling me, that you are relying on."

"Lee, let me ask you if you want to complete it this year, and if so, will you make haste?"

"If I can Yahweh, but can we finish it this year?"

"Yes, it can be done if you apply yourself and do not procrastinate.

"My promise to you reading this is that all who come home to me are blessed and all who do not are to perish. My angels have provided me with all the information necessary to make a decision on who is to be saved and who is not to be, so your pleas are to be heard before the final curtain is drawn.

"My messengers who are alive and living on earth at the moment are waiting to give you directions, and then you will understand why you were born and why you were put on earth, and why you have had to live, and why you have existed in the first place.

"My messengers will give you instructions to follow and then you will find peace and harmony and love, and life fulfilling work. My messengers will give you all the tools you need to work to my plans and your own plans as well.

"My messengers will provide you with instructions on every aspect of life in heaven and on earth, so do not concern yourself that you need to study these things as your studies are to become as one in spirituality, not in physical tasks; and these tasks, though more important to you than you realize, are nowhere near as important as becoming a spiritual being.

"The end result is worth the pain you suffer at the moment with the dreadful reality of death, and the dreadful reality of pain and the dreadful reality of other people; and the dreadful reality of living on earth in these times of trouble, and in times of tribulation and war.

"President Obama has been directed to provide comfort and you have found comfort in hearing great words spoken, so if you are not deaf to him and my messenger, you will have a wonderful life in my presence.

"My messengers are everywhere and some are great and some are not. My plans are to provide you with a comfortable life and if this is not happening, then the world leaders are not doing the right thing and they are to be looked at in the end times. My plans are to have people living in comfort with plenty to eat, without war and without hardship.

"And these hardships you suffer are a direct consequence of your leaders, so look closely at how you perceive leaders to be and make it your priority to have leaders who are fair and not driven by greed, and not driven by power-lust or other unworthy causes.

"Your very existence is due to my having thought of you and if you think it difficult to believe you are one of my thoughts then you are incapable of having everlasting life, as I will not want to have to think about you who denies me and who is not willing to accept that you are made from my thought, not just evolved from a biological phenomenon that is inexplicable to any who studies life on earth.

"And the amount and diversity of life will give you an indication that life was thought out, not just a random happening but well planned and executed as you procreate from each other, making my job easier. And I have to look at more than just procreation, as all is made from the mind and not from the body.

"My plans are that you will accept this and make it possible for me to teach you how to do this in your own world and have your own planets to look after, and you will. And you are going to be in control if you are able to grasp what it is that I am providing you with, in my own way.

"You may think that it is not possible to become a god, who has people created from your own thought, but believe me, I am the proof and have made all of you, so why think you are not able to follow in the footsteps of the creator who is responsible for everything that is?

"Let me add that the way of the living is not the way of the dead. Dead or alive the spirit remains and it is the spirit that is surviving death over the body. The body is a physical shell that is temporary and is changeable too.

"Let me guess your destiny now and you will be able to give yourself a starting chance at what your life will be like next time round, and if you are true to yourself you will be able to adjust, and if you adjust to the climate you may inherit the world.

"Let me add that if you adjust and inherit the world then your father and mother may also inherit what you have found, and that is the love of God, and they will be well provided for in the heat of the moment.

"Let me say how much I wish I had made man in my image and not in the image of Satan, as he is the mold most have finished up as, and I wish it was in the image I intended, not in the image of a male or female that is not worthy of living the life I have provided.

"My messenger has been at the task of writing this, my word, on and off for many years and has not involved himself fully at any time. And he has not been keen to write it lest it bring ridicule and humility upon him and his immediate family.

"My word will bring shame and humility upon the heads of millions but not on the head of my messenger. My wrath is for those he writes this for and not for those listening to me and my angels, and my word will resound in your ears as well.

"Thank you, Yahweh."

"Let me resume from yesterday and today we will progress onto the three houses of the light so far not mentioned in any depth.

"The houses are more complex than you realize as each has to be thought of in a way that it is another country with other languages and other cultures, and other peoples inhabiting them.

"My houses are to bring you into a realm of reality that is to bring you to understand the people's viewpoint from the perspective of happiness and sadness that has permeated your many lives.

"And your heart will be broken many times over in all of these houses as you will recall your past and you will recall the times when you could have made more happen but let it go, as you felt it was unattainable then.

"My messenger is happy to write now as he has met a person he told of the promises of the election in the USA. And all he told her has been forthcoming. And she spoke to him saying her illnesses had miraculously been healed and now she feels better than ever.

"My messenger has felt that this re-enforcement of his prophetic ability has been important to bring him to complete this work I am providing for providence.

"My messenger has been told by this woman who was diagnosed with Hepatitis C and other problems including a cancerous tumor that all evidence of the diseases is now gone. And even blood tests are negative and her life is assured.

"My messenger asked her if anybody had been praying for her, and yes, her sisters were praying. So it has been seen by my messenger that my words are not only words; they are the truth and the light.

"My words make healing happen. And if my messenger asks me to heal somebody, I will endeavor to do so and if he asks me to help someone, I will endeavor to help.

"Let me assure you that praying is the best way to ask me to heal your friends and family. And asking for them to be healed by me is the only way. I have provided you with a self healing spirit from my Holy Spirit and it is a part of me that is in you giving you life. And the healing is also a part of me that is in you.

"I am in you as you have been told by many and that is true, but not in the way they describe it to you at all. My presence in you is my Holy Spirit, which is your soul too. And my Holy Spirit is in my messenger to give you all some encouragement as well as life.

"My messenger has more to offer you than I can give you personally as he is flesh, whereas I am spirit and I am in your life in spirit until you and I are together once more in my house, the House of God.

"My messenger will describe each house to you until you are able to recognize them and when you arrive in one you will be told which house you are in.

"My messenger will give you a description to let you understand your obligations to me here in the light. And he will let you understand that you are to be given the ultimate help in finding your proper level in the light. And all the information you need will be provided for you in the light.

"My messenger will bring you to see me once you are established and you have been able to ascertain your relationship with me and your relationship with my Son.

"My Son is the only one who can give you permission to enter my house, the House of God, and he is the only one authorized to do so. No other person, messenger, prophet or sage or any type of religious man or woman has this authority.

"Only my Son you know as Jesus Christ has this authority. No religion is in my Son and no religion has claim to him who is sent to save you. And none of the established religions have the right to own him or say he is entirely theirs as they are not able to take him from me.

"My messenger will give you all the information you need to quell any misunderstandings and fears you may have if you are not a Christian. My Son is my Son, the Christ or the Messiah that was sent to bring you to salvation.

"My messenger will tell you that he is not going to be responsible for you if you are not willing to let go of your beliefs and take on board that my Son is the key to eternal life and no other. My Son will supply you with all your needs and all you need to know.

"My Son is the most powerful man that ever lived and his word is [the same as] my word. I am not my Son and my Son is not me. We think alike and have the same agenda. We are one in that.

"Let me assure you, we are as one in our thinking and doing so we are as one in all ways as we have designed you and all that is visible to you. And though we have not been visible to you, you have been visible to us.

"We have not made you in our image out of mischief but out of good intention. And we have made you into more than any other animal on earth because we have thought about this for millions of years. And we then decided to make you to work to our plans and our desires.

"Life on earth is not important as you have found and life is relatively shortened if it is not carefully catered for in all manner of ways. And we are thinking how fragile men and women are compared to the spirit world where death is impossible, unless we alone decide to extinguish you.

"And we alone have been responsible for this life you have now and we alone are responsible for the outcome of your existence. Let me assure you that your life in heaven is heavenly and not hard to bear at all. And it will be heaven to be here as well, as you have been told.

"My messenger will inform you that your life in heaven is to be the best life of all you have ever lived through as it is to be the last life you will have, and the last life will be the best life of all.

"My messenger will inform you that you are to have this reward until you do not want it any longer and then you can decide on other ventures of spiritual advancement, other than creative ones.

"My messenger is going to provide you with an itinerary to follow. And if you succeed in the following itinerary you are to be in charge of your own destiny and you are to be given the power to create all you want to, and it will be seen as the most incredible experience in all of your lifetimes and in my lifetime as well. And it will be the first time in history that you, as my beloved creation, apart from procreating, will have produced other worlds from your own mind.

"And you will be able to produce as much as you feel like producing, and my messenger will be watching over it all to overview your progress on these ventures.

"My messenger will be nearby for you to ask information from. And if you have any problems he will sort them out and provide answers to any queries you may have, and all will go smoothly for you in your new role as the creator and god of your own realm.

"Let me assure you reading my prophet's words here today that Yahweh, the living God of Israel, is doing the thinking behind these words and I alone am able to give you eternal life.

"And I alone am able to promise these blessings on your soul, and I alone am able to make life worthy of living. And I alone am here to watch you live your life, and I alone am going to be in charge of your life. And I alone am going to be the one who is making this happen, so in all of your lives, past or present, no matter how important you think yourself to be, none is as important as my Son.

"And no matter if your ego tells you it is not possible for me to give you this in writing, I promise you that your life is in my hands and your life is to be judged according to your heart as well as your hands.

"My messenger wonders if the previous American president is the most evil man alive, but it is not true. Hitler was worse and more lives were lost under his reign than under the rule of the President who sat in church singing hymns while his warplanes bombed the hapless people of Iraq. They are ruthless and are in my Book of Life to be dealt with.

"My created beings will applaud this and will enjoy seeing the last of these men who have wreaked havoc in my world. And these men will be judged and reap the rewards they so much deserve.

"Hitler died in 1945 and his soul still remains alive in the waiting room to be judged. And that is why I have said he is the most evil man alive, though to you he is departed.

"This is how I work and all will see what the ultimate punishment is going to be for these men on Judgment Day. I dislike ruthlessness and they are the worst of the worst. My angels will provide me with their history and I will look over it during the day as well as during the night.

"My messenger sleeps at night but we here in the light do not ever sleep, as why sleep if there is no need to do so? My American friends pray to me to give them freedoms [of choice] and benefits so far denied them and I have listened, awaiting the time to place them in front of the world, and set them free.

"My angels have worked tirelessly to bring about changes in people and in their thought processes that deny them the freedom to think about others in the same way they think about themselves, and their immediate families.

"My plans are to bring all decent people together in one big united family and have all working alongside each other in harmony to be at the forefront of creation. And all will enjoy this experience immensely, and all of you will be creative once you have my full approval; and to gain my approval you must first be enlightened.

"After entering the light at the Level of Introduction you will learn that life is not over at all but is a long term plan for mankind, to give you the opportunity to grow spiritually and emotionally.

"My messenger has been able to gain spiritual enlightenment by passing many tests whilst living on earth, and has been told he has to be better than others to live in my house with me, at the time of judgment.

"He has often forgone his pact because he has sinned many times and I have forgiven him. But now he sins daily and finds himself in dire straights because he wants more than he is entitled to have.

"My covenant with him was to write my words down, but only recently has he obliged me and done what he has been asked to do. And only recently has he been reinstated to his former position, and carries my banner with him too.

"My messenger has had to go through many tests. And he started off at the Level of Introduction to learn the ropes, and was quickly promoted to the Level of Higher Learning.

"It was at the Level of Introduction he learned how to ignite my passion and found he was able to communicate with the spirits of the dead.

"My messenger found the Level of Settlement to be the most populated in the light and discovered his past there, as many of his ancestors reside there.

"My messenger discovered that his ancestors were from nearly all religions and from many races in Europe. And he discovered that all people enjoy living there and are given information pertaining to their spiritual growth and development, although it is far from the amount of spiritual enlightenment that they will finally attain.

"The Level of Competence is where you will discover more about yourself than you have ever previously known. You will find manual tasks to do as well as mental stimulation here and will enjoy both.

"And here you will learn how to do many tasks you had no idea about when you were on earth, and you will find that you walked about with your eyes shut and your mind closed.

"You will see for the first time how people made their products and you will see how some were able to make magnificent objects of incredible beauty such as the frescoes and statues that once lined the streets of ancient cities. And they were able to produce these with their nimble fingers and agile minds.

"People without these special skills took up other work where manual dexterity was not expected of them. At this level, the Level of Competence, unskilled people will learn how to use their hands in conjunction with their heads.

"My plan is that you will be brought up to a level of competence that will be necessary to produce anything you require for your future. And all knowledge to do so will be given freely to you for the duration of your practical learning experience here.

"Once you have mastered your practical skills you will be ready to enter the Level of Enlightenment. This level is the highest level possible for most of you as only those selected for higher learning can proceed beyond this point.

"The Level of Higher Learning is where the faithful few will wait in preparation for entry into my personal house after Judgment.

"Let me add that I am the God who is to take you into my heart and into my house, and you are the servant of the Angel of Divinity who is to look into your heart, and into your house.

"My angels are everywhere and your spirit guides are with you most of the time. My angels will require you to perform miracles and you will require your angels to perform miracles as well. My messenger is going to tell you how many angels are looking after you and how many guides you have.

"My beloved Son will provide you with all the information you need to enter my domain and he will let you in and seat you directly in front of me, to give you firsthand experience in the House of God.

"And you will be soothed by his presence and will be told to remain with him until you are judged and have found your rightful place.

"My Son is to provide you with comfort and give you my word to read, and he will provide you with the key to my house as well. And he will introduce you to my angels and will fold the cloth and wipe the table, and he will pour the wine and give you bread to eat, and he will wash your feet and comb your hair as well, as he will want you to be comfortable here. And he will make you feel most welcome and keep you entertained for as long as he can.

"Let me reassure you that your life is to be wonderful and not full of stress or anxiety, and your time is to be your own and you can pursue any activity you want to.

"My Son will give you any advice on anything you need to know as he is full of information. And he has been studying all of these things for centuries, and knows more about them than anybody else on my earth.

"Let me tell you too that your life is in the hands of my Son so do not take your own life by denying him his. Let me remind you that your life is in my care and my Son is your carer.

"My life is my own and your life is my own as well, so do not forget that without my guidance and my help you have nobody else to take my place, and nobody else is capable of doing the things I am able to do.

"My beloved Son is here to apply my principles to your life on earth and to your life after death. My Son will take his time to explain it to you in detail and go over the details with you for as long as you want to, for you to learn what you need to know and understand, in my realms.

"My universal understanding is involved with a lot of intricate detail and your earthly understanding is involved with a lot of intimate detail. You will learn much more here than you did on earth and you will be required to pursue knowledge. And this knowledge will be provided to you by my Son and his helpers.

"Let me remind you too that your time is forever, not to be wasted but to be fruitful. And you will be rewarded for your efforts here and you rewards will be bountiful, and you will cherish all of them.

"My beloved Son is to provide you with many of these gifts as well and he will provide you with all of your needs, whether you need them or not.

"Let me also tell you that if you require more than he has to offer you will be given it, whatever it is, as you are special and unique in that you are here in my house. And to have been placed here without hindrance of any type is to be loved by me, and you will have proven to me that you deserve this privilege.

"My Son will provide you with whatever you want regardless of what it is and you will receive anything you ask for, and you will be given as much as your heart desires.

"My Son is to be standing by your side to make you happy and to provide you with this happiness.

"My Son will take his time to explain this situation and to give you the reason he is your helper rather than you helping him. My Son has more power than any other living being and he will prevail whereas all others will falter.

"And once here in my house, you will find my Son has taken hold of your life and turned it around so that you are still living in death, and if you think that it is not possible, then ask anyone here and you will realize that my word is the word of the living God.

"My wish is that you are capable of reaching the Level of Enlightenment as this is the hardest level for any of my earthly children to grasp, as the enlightened are able to converse with me.

"My Son will provide you with updates on just about anything you will need to know and have here. My helpers will give you the necessary equipment to harvest the crops and plant the seeds for the next harvest.

"Let me add that if you wish to defy me in that you do not want any of these blessings, then it is your punishment that you have none of them and miss out on them. And once you have decided that you are worthy of taking my gifts, they are yours to keep, not mine.

"If you wish to discard them you may do so, but remember they are not easily regained, and those of you who throw them away will no longer be entitled to all that you were born to have.

"All are born to have, but most fall by the wayside. Be grateful if you have reached the Level of Higher Learning as from here eternal life in my house is assured you.

"My personal house, the House of God is where the angels who look after you on a daily basis and their brethren will reside after the judgment.

"All the houses of angels will be empty and all will remain empty if you are to be saved, as you will require the angels to look after you in the heavenly realms you reside in, eventually.

"No matter on which level you reside at, the angels will be here to keep the harmony and have everyone producing the goods and chattels you deem necessary to provide comfort, and these products will be plentiful.

"My houses in the light are all different with many places and all have different landscapes with different views to look at, and all have different plants and all have different animals as well.

"All will be a paradise and all will provide you with the necessities you need for the time you reside there.

"All have to be cleaned and all have to be washed and polished too, so you will discover many talents in that area of life and that is, the cleaner you live, the closer to my heart you will reside.

"My messenger is cleaner than you are at the moment as he is purer in thought, word and deed.

"My messenger is having trouble with the people on earth and is amazed at how selfish and unkind they are. And he wishes it was not like this and will treat them all according to how he perceives them, and how they behave themselves toward him.

"My messenger is excited over the prospect of finishing this project as he sees it is close to completion. And after it is completed I will bring many angels with me to earth and start the process of judging the dead, and he will be here with me helping out, as well.

"My angels will give the dead their final judgment day and they will all be in line waiting for this, their final judgment.

"My messenger will help hand out the judgments with me and my Son. And he will help me with the difficult ones and he will give me the time to ponder over the requirements of the many; and he will help in difficult decision making as he has a strong will and is against capital punishment.

"Let me remind you that the judgment leads either to eternal life or eternal death, and this final punishment is far worse than being electrocuted in an electric chair or swinging by the neck on the end of a rope, until dead.

"Let me remind you that your life is not to be judged by people you know but by my Son and my messengers, and all the angels will contribute with their particular knowledge of your good deeds.

"Good works and good deeds are the key to eternal life and if you have shunned them, you will be shunned too.

"My angels provide you with information all day and night to do the deeds necessary to make life bearable for millions of people who are involved in your life, in some important way. And you are to be held responsible for your own words and deeds toward them all.

"My messenger has provided me with the details of the lives of many and I have looked closely at their lives under the magnificent microscope of the universe that is my pleasure to have.

"And I have mimicked their antics to see what has motivated them and have discovered what was going on in their minds when they were acting out their actions and doing their deeds.

"So if you are thinking you are not doing any deeds of good will, you may be wrong as good deeds are also in your head and only need to be made into physical reality by the donation of money to a good charity that will then provide relief to the needy.

"Good works are the works of my angels and good works and deeds are done by both men and angels alike. Good works are the crucial part of living that combines you to me and without good works, nothing is accomplished.

"Nothing will likewise be rewarded with the end result that no-one has been saved and none are here to enjoy the fruits laid out for you.

"Let it remain then, that to be rewarded you must do good in the world and the way to do good is to do good works and good deeds.

"Let me reiterate that in yet another way. If you plan on entering my house you must know how to do manual work. And if you do not then you will receive no heavenly rewards, as all you will produce in my house will be from your own work. And if you have nothing to show, it will be because you have done nothing.

"My messenger has spent his whole life learning skills to provide himself and others with happiness, and he is able to do things that would otherwise be out of his reach, moneywise.

"And he has these skills because he learned them and now he uses them day and night. He is now able to do many good works and good deeds and provide money to the needy. And he does work for the needy as well.

"You have to provide others with money to be considered for entry into heaven, and if you have been a selfish person, not giving help to people in need then you will find no-one is going to help you.

"You cannot buy your way in here by making donations to your church or doing deeds for your congregation. You need to help those in need in the world, not those in your own home as this is not charity to the people but is charity to those in your family circle, and that is not the charity I need here.

"My messenger has been thinking about this as he has provided help to hundreds. And his church told him to pray and not do any good works as good works were the work of the Catholic faith alone, not the protestant faith.

"This has been misconstrued, as good works during the time of the German theologian, Martin Luther, were to raise money to build the Vatican. And this money raised by selling indulgences was intended for the house of worship only and was not raised by unscrupulous means but by charitable men who gave freely. And as a token of their generosity the church provided them with a token gesture of securing a place in my house.

"No-one believed these indulgences were fact at the time as they were merely a token of gratitude shown by the church elders, used to promote the cause of building a house of worship.

"So take it from me, the God who is in heaven and on earth, that you will be rewarded for doing good works as well as doing good deeds.

"Let me add that if you believe you can buy yourself a place in heaven then you are not giving yourself any credibility. And if you believe the people living in those times of trouble were less than you are, then you are not giving them any credibility either.

"Prayers are only answered by my angels if they see the recipient is God loving and is genuine and is of good spiritual character or is the parent of a child in need.

"Let me add that all those with a face to making money are not as spiritual as those with a cause and if the cause is for the good of mankind then they are in front of the others spiritually as well as being my friends.

"My people are also going to have the money needed to buy the necessities of life, not the luxuries that I will bestow on them here; as the others, who have purchased all that money can buy; will not be here to get them from me, and not be invited in anyway.

"My angels see that these people have what they need on earth now, and they oversee it properly that they have a good innings, as it is the last innings for them, not the beginning as it is for my children.

"Let me remind you too that you are to be here with me and this is the highest place that I can place you, in my arms and in my heart.

"And any who are here are blessed in all ways, not just blessed but honored as well, as the highest honor is to be here in my house.

"My angels are all here in my arms as they are the highest ranking over all the earth. And the universe has many forms of life in it.

"And the universe has many forms of spiritual entities looking after it. And the angels are all spiritual entities, and they are all here to be thanked and to be honored. And they have to be seen and they have to be given their rewards too.

"My messenger is to be rewarded in another way, and that is he will oversee most of the building and manufacturing processes.

"He will oversee it all and he will be here to give advice and to be asked how it all goes together, and he will give you the answers;

and he will give you all the information you need to do the job at hand.

"My presence will also be felt at these times and you will know that my presence is in you too, as you will feel my power in all you undertake.

"And all you accomplish will seem surreal as you will have it done in less time than it takes on earth. And you will be astonished at how quickly your thoughts become reality, and all you think is going to become a reality, will.

"My own mind has produced countless billions of objects that are still in the process of manufacture and will still take millions of years to complete. My experiment with mankind was very fruitful and has invigorated me and has given me more food for thought.

"And it has been the reason I am going to give you another chance after your life here on earth, and it is the reason you are going to be allowed into my house.

"Let me also say that you are to be relished here by me. And you will see for yourself that you have been selected by me through my Son and my messengers who are to divide the spoils of goodness with you, and show you the ropes.

"My Son will show you how to use your gifts; and only then will you realize all you have inherited here, in this, my kingdom. And this kingdom will be yours to have, and you will become as one in your thinking and your love. And you will then realize just how important love and compassion is; as how can you create it, without it?

"My Son is the one to show you how to manage things here, and you will learn more than you have previously known before even though you may be brilliant in your field, as you have only been told what you know by men.

"And here you are to be told by me. And no-one will deny the truth to you and no-one here will lie to you and no-one here will gild the lily, as all knowledge will be authentic and not copied from Satan's handbook.

"My thoughts are that you will begin life here with so much in front of you that you will be overwhelmed with it all; but it will soon become apparent to you that your life is forever, and all that is in front of you is to be taken gradually; not rushed, and why rush?

"Nothing is forever except you and me, so be told, take it easy and relax. No-one will be behind you urging you on and no-one will be making you do anything you do not wish to do or making you do anything you are not keen on; and no-one will make you participate in anything uncongenial to you, either.

"My Son will allow you into my presence and you may be able to stay with me for a time until you are self sufficient and have a full grasp of what is happening, and what is required of you to be one of the masters of the universe.

"And my Son will tell you time and time again that if you create trouble for yourself then you can handle it, as you can stop what you have started, at anytime.

"And when it is apparent that you are ready, I will supervise you personally for the time it takes you to grasp the responsibilities that go along with being at one with me in my house, in thought, word and deed.

"And you alone will be the one responsible for your actions from thereon in, as you and you alone will have the full authority to do anything you want to do, without redress of any type.

"And no-one will tell you that you can or cannot do a certain task or make a certain project or create a new form of life or create new life, and no-one will dare say that you are wrong as it will result in them being chastised by you, as well as by me.

"Let me ask you all if you wish to learn more about me or not? If so, then why do you deny I exist in the world?

"Let me ask you if you think you have been ignored by me? If so, then why are you here reading my word?

"Let me ask you if you think you are special in my eyes? Let me assure you that you are and that your life is going to change dramatically once you are here, to be given the gifts I have made ready for you in my house. And you will relish them for you are to be seen with me in the house, and you are to be seen in the house without me as well.

"My presence is not going to make you a better person spiritually, it is the reason you are born to be tested in ongoing ways to ascertain your spiritual beliefs and strengths, so be told that your spiritual beliefs are going to be tested to the maximum and your personality will show through here in my house.

"My messenger will provide you with all the spiritual guidance you need, to be accepted in the long run. And if you have any difficulties accepting the ways of my messenger then you will be told that you are to be given some extra tuition, to instill in you the understanding that comes from faith and the strength to accept that my faith in you is the main reason you are to be given this privilege.

"My messenger will provide you with the time and the place to do your research into the role you are to play, and the role you will have, and this role is the role of living in the house in my name, and you will relish this privilege as well.

"My messenger will provide you with more than enough information to make it happen and you will, so be proud of that. Be told that it will happen to you regardless of your beliefs at the moment, as you will undertake higher learning to give you an education and to give you an understanding, and to give you all you require to know, to have everlasting life and untold powers.

"Your existence will be peaceful and only those with peaceful hearts and minds will be asked to enter the house to be given the keys to eternal life, and the power to have the universe run to your beck and call.

"My angels will be helping you in your progression and you will grow in time into my image as you have been told over and over to the tune of inundation, and you will realize that my word is worthy of your ears and your words are worthy of mine.

"My realization about the serenity and the selflessness in your heart is why you are to be given the opportunity to be the one and only gift to my angels, and they will see you are the reward they have prayed for.

"And your reward will be to take the angels into your heart and have them bless you and have them take instructions from you, and have them all believing your word is the word of a living god and the word of my own design.

"My angels will provide you with as much as you require and more, and they will work tirelessly for you, and they will be unpaid as none will accept payment for working in my name; and none are to be rewarded with earthly gifts as I have rewards of a heavenly nature stored up in my bank, and my bank has no vaults or safes and no-one can be told what is in there.

"My angels will find out in their own time and they will see their rewards are not the rewards that men seek but the rewards that I bestow, and you will all know then that I am the one and only God and you will then understand what is meant by, My Word and My Way.

"My image will be as an old man but my strength will be as a lion, and my way of truth will be as a granite wall of gigantic proportions, and you will be unable to climb over it without my assistance.

"My messenger will not thwart you in anyway as men thwart you and my messenger will be here to provide you with assistance as you need it. And you will find that you progress rapidly in your spiritual pursuits and those pursuits are to be given to you, and you will gain knowledge thus untold and thus hidden and thus unavailable to anyone, except to my Son.

"My messenger is not going to finish this work unless he is rewarded, and he will get his reward as I have made a covenant with him, and he will rejoice and be happier than he has ever been in his entire life.

"And he will find a happiness that has been denied him so far. And he has lived a life of happy and sad memories, but this last part of his life is to be my reward, and this will be final.

"Let it be known that he is in my house as my messenger, not as an intruder in the house or as an unwanted guest but as the messenger, and the Holy Spirit in him will provide me with my reward.

"My goal is to make you all happy and you will be happier than ever before, so be happy in this knowledge and rejoice that your life is to be rewarded with many things, to make it worth living.

"And you will then understand why your life was so hard in the beginning, and how difficult it has been for me to see you wallow in doubt, despair and anguish.

"And you have been punished by people who are themselves to be punished and you will see all of them perish in the hellfire, and you will rejoice at their plight too.

"Let me add that you are to be rewarded for the efforts you have put into people's lives on earth.

"And even though they have smacked your face in return by their ingratitude, they have been helped with the issues bothering them, and even though they have bitten the hand that fed them, they have been helped to survive and made into better people.

"My angels and my messenger are here to help them, but remember that my messenger is visible and is in front of them and can tell them exactly what is going on in the world of spirits, and the world of angels.

"My stages of existence are varied and yours are varied as well. You will be finding out the reason why you exist and you will discover more, as you seek more.

"And the answers to all of your questions will be given to you and the results of all your lives will be told. And the time of your being born is in my palm, to be advised to you, and your life which is in the palm of my hand is to be shown to you.

"And the way of your life is to be expressed in the best possible manner and the findings are to be told to the world. And your life is to be exposed and your thoughts will be visible, as they have substance and cannot be destroyed by any but me and my angels.

"My angels will destroy your thoughts only under my instructions and they will guide you and give you new thinking skills. And you will discover that you have more thinking skills here in my house than you have ever had at anytime on earth, as it will instigate full knowledge and understanding and full hindsight and full foresight and insight into all that you ever knew, or will ever need to know."

"Yahweh, where do the nine houses of angels fit in here?"

"Lee, the nine houses of angels are adjacent to the five levels of the light, on the same plane but separated by my presence until the day of resurrection and the subsequent judgment of all entities."

"Yahweh, will this information you are giving me cause people to become angry if it is not what they want to see or hear?"

"You will be attacked by all and sundry, but ignore them as they will find out the truth eventually."

"Yahweh, why is all this flurry of activity going on in the nine celestial houses lately?"

"We are living in the last days and before long, judgment will begin. This is known as Judgment Day, but will actually take over one thousand years to complete."

"Yahweh, how will those who are dead, buried or cremated return in their bodies?"

"The bodies of the dead are rotted or destroyed by fire or other means and they are gone forever. The resurrected will be in spirit until the Day of Judgment and they will appear in a glorified body and this will be similar to having a body but not a physical body. And even those souls living in hell as orbs of energy will be embodied like this, for the judgment.

"This empyreal body could be regarded as a hologram and the resurrected will not physically touch or move solid objects with this celestial body."

"Is this body temporary or is it what we will remain with, Yahweh?"

"Lee, this embodiment is temporary; it is not permanent and will be different, and I have other plans for them. All people have had numerous bodies and the body at the time of resurrection will be the last body image they recall. And this body is to be discarded as soon as their judgment is over.

"And all living during this time will remain in their body and will remain on earth until such time as they need to return to their heavenly home, which is the proper place to be. And they will simply ask me to take them home and leave the earth altogether.

"All those resurrected will either enter my kingdom or perish after judgment and punishment and those resurrected, upon entering my kingdom will have a choice of returning to earth again, as those born of woman.

"And they will be immortal, not having the curse of death on their heads, and all of them will have as much time on their hands as is conceivable. And all of them will be able to transfer from one reality to the other and be able to return to the spiritual world at will.

"They will all return to my kingdom without their physical bodies, discarding them as a moth discards a cocoon."

"Yahweh, after judgment, will those few entering your house, the Kingdom of God, have a physical body or a spiritual body?"

"Let me say that it will be both as the body has no limitations. All the angels will have both physical and spiritual bodies, so be told this and be told that all will have beautiful bodies, as I want all to be proud of their countenance.

"And this is to be their reward and this body is to be surrounded with my light. And this aura will appear to some as a halo, but in truth it is a field of energy at a high level of light, and it is beautiful to behold and all will be like this."

"Yahweh, what is the difference between this present life and the one after the resurrection?"

"Lee, all people will have a choice of being in the spiritual world or in the physical world without the fear of dying and they can stay for as long as they like in one or the other.

"Presently, [in modern times] the people who have died number nearly twice the amount of people living right now, and the present population on earth is getting close to seven billion.

"Each soul progresses through many lives and the total number of lives each person has, varies, many being newly created for this life whereas others such as yourself have lived numerous times before, your soul being many thousands of years old."

"Yahweh, why can't I remember any of my previous lives?"

"The lives you have lived are all remembered; it is that the physical brain you were born with in this life does not store these memories as it is a new body, and the brain has not been exposed to any prior knowledge."

"Yahweh, can I ever access the memories of a past life?"

"Of course you can, and the memories are all there for you when you become a spirit being again, as all the memories are available to you once you leave the physical body and become a non-physical entity which is the natural state; the physical body being my gift to you for a short time, then the body is returned to me.

"The physical body is a state of temporary being, letting the body have its free will on earth until I call it home for other duties, or to keep the human race on its path as I have destined, whereas the spiritual body or state is a permanent one.

"I do not see death as a tragedy or loss as you do but merely a transition from one state to another. In reality it is a progression and if people were aware of what was in store for them, they would regard death as something to be looked forward to.

"It will be more than you expect as all previous lives lived will be returned in full memory for you to relish and enjoy. My angels will tell you what you have done and you will recall it all in full detail too. And all of your previous lives will be returned to you in full."

"Yahweh, at present the angels in the light help people whenever they can and also keep the planet safe, and the angels entering your house after judgment will be allowed to create new life. Can you give me more information about them and their roles?"

"Lee, the Nine Celestial Houses are full of angels, guardian angels and archangels. All have differing roles and all are to be rewarded by me at the time of judgment for their services to humanity.

"After judgment, human spirits entering any of my houses as

angels will be on the same level as my existing angels. My existing angels, who have not ever been human beings, have been loyal and deserve the same chance of gaining access to my personal house, known as the Kingdom of God, as any human has.

"And the majority of human spirits, as angels and all existing angels will still remain in the light, that is, in my houses of heaven, at their designated level, not being given access to my personal house and the reason is this:

"Eventually they will grow in spiritual matters and will have been schooled in the house of Higher Learning, and more will then be allowed in, to take up the responsibilities that go with more power and more knowledge.

"All living with me and my Son in my personal house, the Kingdom of God, will become as I am, and they will assume responsibilities that are far greater and more important than the others will have. And this is to be the ultimate reward for my faithful believers in Christ."

THE BODY OF CHRIST

"Yahweh, can you give me a description of your Son, Jesus of Nazareth, so we may glean an idea of what he actually looked like? The only description we have of him is by the prophet Isaiah who described him as disfigured and marred." (Isaiah 52:14)

"I will give you the statistical information and the rest is up to the imagination, but the statistics are accurate and any who read can start to see him.

"My Son was a tall man for his time as he stood 5'-9" tall, (175 cm) weighed 161Lb. (75 kg) and was well defined muscularly. He kept physically fit by walking everywhere, not overindulging in food, eating only once daily and sometimes only every second day.

"His countenance was that of a handsome man and his physical presence was very much that of a man who was from another time and place. He had black hair that came down to his shoulders and his eyebrows and beard were also black.

"His eyes were dark brown and his appearance was that of a man who stayed outdoors in the fresh air and sunshine. Dark skinned and tanned all over with a healthy complexion; he kept his body in peak physical condition.

"The Apostles were also in peak condition due to the walking and the exercise they had during the day.

"My Son looked and was an exceptional man with a high forehead and a striking presence, exuding power and authority. He was described as being the perfect man by those who knew him personally.

"Let me say this to you. My Son was treated badly and beaten brutally before he died. Let me say that he was disfigured and marred by the treatment he received at the hands of his captors.

"And my love for my Son differs from the love you have for your son as my love is forever and all encompassing whereas the love you have for your son is fickle, transitional and temporary!

"And why do you say this [communion] cup contains the blood of my Son? And why do you say this bread is the body of my Son?

"This was a direction to my Son's disciples to partake of the bread and the wine in memory of his life on earth and the fulfillment of his covenant with me, (Matthew 26: 26-28) not a direction to make it into a three-ringed circus with many interpretations and many names and many traditions springing out of these words given to future generations who do not even realize what is truly meant.

"And any who believe in me and my Son are his disciples. And all people who believe in him are welcome to commemorate his life by drinking from the cup of life and eating of the bread of life.

"My Son sits with me in my house, [the Kingdom of God] and is with me in my house. My Son is not residing in the body of the multitudes, the gathered community of believers that drink and eat the communion breakfast, and it is false to teach this.

"They have their own lives with their own bodies and their own flesh and blood, so why would I give them the flesh and blood of my Son as well?

"This ceremony is due to the words of my Son being taken literally and you all know he spoke in parables to the multitudes and to his disciples, to make them think.

"My Son can communicate his thoughts to my enlightened messengers who are spiritually aware, and I do this too. My thoughts are constantly being impressed into the minds of my messengers who do my will and who are my willing servants.

"And he said this to the apostles as he wanted the apostles to commemorate his life, not the future here and now but the future they had then."

> 26 While they were eating, Jesus took a loaf of bread, and after blessing it he broke it, gave it to the disciples, and said, "Take, eat; this is my body." 27 Then he took a cup, and after giving thanks he gave it to them, saying, "Drink from it, all of you; 28 for this is my blood of the covenant, which is poured out for many for the forgiveness of sins. 29 I tell you, I will never again drink of this fruit of the vine until that day when I drink it new with you in my Father's kingdom."
> (Matthew 26: 26-29) NRSV

"Feel free to take communion, but remember it is for the reason of remembering his life, not to think he is part of you because of some mistaken idea you have. And this is still wine from the grape or the substitute you have for it.

"And remember too that my Son will drink this new wine and eat this bread with you in my house in my kingdom if you are here, and he is not going to be eating or drinking his own flesh and blood.

"It is not the blood of my Son but a fluid substance in memory of his spilt blood and the bread is not the flesh of my Son, but the bread is the bread of life from the resurrection and this is to commemorate his resurrection, as well as his life.

"And now you say it is for the purpose of having his presence, the Body of Christ in you; the chosen ones, who make this mistake!

"And you are too ready to believe this nonsense that I have chosen you above the millions of others who believe in me and my beloved Son!

"Feel free to do this [take communion] in my name and the name of my Son and of my Holy Spirit that gave you life, because my Son is part of the universe as you are. And all that is, is of and from me who created you, so take this to think over now.

"And some of you from the Christian church are wrong in thinking that because you are the Body of Christ as one faithful community of believers, you are in me and I am in you, as I am my Son in the flesh and he is me in Spirit, which is not the case at all.

"This is derived from the New Testament where my Son was deliberately misinterpreted, saying, 'I and the Father are one,' (John 10:30) NIV, and the true meaning of the words my Son conveyed to the crowd is, 'I and my father are *as* one.'"

> John 10: **29** *"What my Father has given me is greater than all else, and no-one can snatch it out of the Father's hand."* **30** *"The Father and I are one."* **31** *The Jews took up stones again to stone him.* **32** *Jesus replied, "I have shown you many good works from the Father."* NRSV

"This was not what was intended, that he be me in the flesh. It is not true at all; he is my Son, he is not me.

"Let me say this to you; you will soon find out who you really are when I look into your hearts and minds! And if you are still deluded, then you will be asked to state where you are going to reside!

"And if you are misguided enough to tell me that you are going to reside in the Kingdom of God because you are one of the gathered community of faithful believers, then you will soon find out that you are indeed one of the faithful few who get left out in the cold, as you have believed the rants and ravings of a few overzealous fools who have distorted the truth about your birth right!

"And this birth right is to believe in me and my Son and the Holy Spirit that gave you the breath of life. And if you who come from my breath are including yourself as the inner self that is me then you are to be advised again that you are flesh and blood and I am God, not flesh and blood like you.

"So how can you be in me if you have flesh and blood and I am Spirit? And how can you say with full confidence that you are in me and I am in you?

"Perform a few miracles such as reviving the dead and shifting the desert sands; or shifting all the buildings [as in earthquakes or cyclones] as Satan does, whenever I let him out of my sight, then.

"Let me dispel this other myth too, that your church is my house. My house is in heaven and the church is a body of people living on earth who worship me and my Son.

"Let it be known now that all believers are part of the church in my Son's name and this church is the body of people who love him and love me, who created all things.

"And all who enter my house in heaven will be invited in after they have proven themselves worthy. And all who think it will be too difficult to prove themselves are wrong as I love all of my children. And all that is required to come home to me, your loving Father, is to ask to be forgiven, and you will be.

"And all believers are members of the church of Christ as all denominations are one church, [one body of believers] the church of Christ. And all [who are to be saved] will be part of this church before they can be called home to be judged, if they want to be part of my plan.

"It is not necessary to be baptized in the name of the Father, Son and Holy Ghost to be a member of my church as baptism was reserved for the Jewish disciples in the days of my Son on earth.

"And I made it clear my Son was also baptized as an example to the other disciples. And that part of me you refer to as the Holy Ghost was not known to his disciples or the multitudes in those times.

"This baptism was to show him the people were prepared to follow his path, and they did. Let it be known he was the most sought after man in the vicinity of Palestine and Israel then.

"To show my Son that you follow his path it is only necessary to be present in front of him in church as he knows your mind, and it is not necessary to be immersed in water to prove you are worthy.

"A small ceremony by human hands will not get you into my house and to think so is foolish as I decide who comes in, and a small ceremony held by man will not turn my face toward you.

"The key to my house is for you to be forgiven of your sins and only then will you be allowed into my house. My Son and my anointed servants will be the decision makers here as they hold the key, not men or women in charge of ceremonies held on earth in my name and in the name of my Son.

"Let me remind you this is the truth, and the way into my house and my heart is to follow my word in this, my last testament, my Gospel to you.

"My messenger is feeling perplexed in writing this down, as he has been told by one denomination of Baptists that to be in their church he must first be baptized and then become a member.

"He has been told that to become a church member he must be baptized as an adult believer, meaning he must be aware of why he is being baptized.

"Only then is he to be allowed to partake of Holy Communion with other members who drink of the wine and eat the bread.

"Then he has been led to believe he is to be part of the gathered community of believers, who are the Body of Christ.

"Let me say this to you who think this! My Son holds the key to my house! Many in the gathered community of believers are not going to enter my house. And if you think you are going to enter because you are my Son in Body, then you have been misled!

"My idea is that if you want to be baptized, please do so in your own time and at your own discretion, but remember this is not necessary to be part of my plan, and that plan is to be in my image creating as I create.

"And this plan does not need a small ceremony in any church to make me turn my head in your direction, and to think so is vanity on your behalf and ego on the behalf of the church leaders.

"Let me make it clear to you, this is in vain as I alone decide if you have been worthy in life to share my house in death. And I alone make the final decision even though my Son gives you entry into my house in heaven.

"My house is my haven, so do you think I want any disruption here in my own sanctuary? No, I do not!

"Do you think me such a kind father that I will allow those who disrupt the plans of mankind to the point where people die from their decisions and have a miserable death and leave broken hearts behind them, into my sanctuary? No! I am not!

"Do you think my head will turn in your direction if you drink wine and eat bread in church, saying it is drinking and eating the flesh and blood of my Son in his memory at the Last Supper?

"And you drink wine and eat bread in the hope it will somehow transform you into a special person worthy of entrance into my house, if you are not? Think again!

"Only those who come to me, my Son or my messengers asking to be forgiven of all their sins will be allowed into my house!

"Let me elaborate on this too in case it is trampled on in a way not intended to be.

"You can ask me to forgive you at any time and at any place, but I will listen more intently to you if you are in a house of worship at the time.

"And I regard any church of Christ as belonging in the House of God, and you will know and I will know that you are genuine.

"I do not usually hear sinners and only those asking to be forgiven will be heard. Your prayers to me are heard by my angels who then supply me with your records, and if you are genuinely sorry then I will forgive you.

"Ask me to forgive you at any time, anywhere, and you will be heard! And to make it clear to me you are genuine you must make the effort to enter my Son's house of worship and say you are sorry there.

"You can confess your sins to a holy man or do it in silent prayer. My angels will listen to you and you will be heard!

"No amount of immersion in water will wash away your sins and no amount of drinking wine and eating bread, for whatever reason or belief you have in this ritual will give you any advantage whatsoever over a person who has come to me and asked to be forgiven.

"Do you think I do not value those who have not been baptized or have not taken Holy Communion?

"If you think this, think again, as the paradise you seek will be a paradise not to your liking, as it will be a fool's paradise.

"Look at the number of people born after Christ who have not been baptized and look at the number of people born before Christ who have not, and see if you can justify leaving them out of my plans, if I see they are worthy.

"And only those who are worthy will be allowed into my house in heaven. And only those in heaven who are seen as the elect will enter my kingdom, the Kingdom of God, from there.

"From [one of] my houses in heaven [the kingdom of heaven] you will be selected [at the time of your Judgment] to enter my kingdom [the Kingdom of God] by my Son and his helpers, as he holds the key, and if I see you are worthy I will let you in.

"Both kingdoms are separate places and both kingdoms are different places and both kingdoms have many realms.

"Let it remain that there is one body of people in this church of Christ and all Christians are free to worship in this one ecumenical church that I want. (Refer to 1 Corinthians12:12)

"No-one is to be regarded as inferior or told that they are not worthy of entering my Son's house on earth, as why would I create you if you are deemed unworthy of me?

"And why would I have you in this house without wanting you?

"Let it remain at the discretion of the pastor or priest to be there for you, not for the church in its entirety but for you alone, as you alone are the one reading this, and you alone are the one to be in front of me to be asked what you have done on earth, and why you feel you are special in my eyes.

"Let me ask you if you can tell me why you should be allowed to enter my kingdom, the Kingdom of God? And if you cannot then you should start thinking about it clearly in the near future, and you should be prepared to answer this in detail too.

"My Son is alive and living and is preparing for his return. And he is trying to decide what he is going to say to the church members.

"And he will address them as one body of members of one united church of Christians, not as Catholics, Anglicans; Lutherans, Greek Orthodox, Seventh Day Adventists or any other number of Christian organizations.

"My Son will address you as fellow Christians in his new reign and he will not be asking you what denomination you are from, rather he will be asking you how much time you spend in church, how much time you spend helping out in the community and how much of your income you give to the poor and needy. (Not church tithes).

"And not in dollars but in percentages, so if he sees you are more generous to other people than yourself he will give you all of your money back in full.

"And he will give you food forever. And he will give you life everlasting. And he will give you his love. And he will give you presents that are invaluable to you. And he will give you anything that you need in your time and place on this earth. And you will be regarded with great esteem in his eyes. And as you regard him, so will he regard you.

"Let it be seen that my messenger Lee has been doing my work in many ways, and he has been instructing some people in spiritual matters. Not the spiritual teachings that the theological colleges and seminaries provide, but in true spiritual matters that are provided by me.

"And he has these gifts to share now and if he wants to divulge them he may do so, and if he does not, that is his prerogative. And all his spiritual teachings are through me, the God who loves you. And he relishes that he is in this position of power in my sight. Let me add that my angels are here to provide you with my wisdom.

"Let me remind all of you my Son is going to make you see the truth before you are allowed into my house. And that truth is for the ones who are spiritually aware of their place in the world.

"No amount of crystals or colors or other nonsense will get you further into the realms of light, so forget that garbage and take up 'The Word' and look at it intently, and take notice of everything that you have been instructed about.

"Let it be seen that I will be the one to chastise you in this as your heart is hard and your mind is set, letting it become an issue that is to be discussed in the House of Higher Learning and it will be.

"Lee will take you to task and his role includes helping Meheliah, the Angel of Death and Darkness rid the world of rubbish. And he will pass the garbage on to my messenger of death and darkness to be extinguished; so be told now you have little time left to make your plans for the future as there will not be one, and you will perish.

"Let it remain we are going to unshackle Satan at the last minute to allow him time to take you with him to his house [the abyss]. And it will be there you will perish with him in the agony you gave me, and this is to be my joy, to have you gone from my sight.

"And you will scream out to be saved but alas, I will not hear you as I am going to be deaf to your noise. And you can get an angel to hear you if you like.

"But it will be like trying to bring fish into the house out of the rain as you will be suffocating in your own filth and vomit. And you will be extinguished over this time, and the time is to be the time that I determine.

"And you will wallow in this squalor, and you will not be able to say anything at all as I have the power to stop you from speaking, and I have the power to stop you from saying or doing anything.

"And I have the power to do anything I want. And this power will be used to extinguish you in the next intake of sinners, as they will die and be buried here in my name, and in the name of my church of faithful believers in Christ.

"My Son will expect that you, in my church of faithful believers will be doing good works as well as being faithful and diligent servants of his. [God does many good works through the Son] (John 10:32)

"And if you think doing good works is above your station in life then you will see just what that means when you are in my presence. And you will understand that doing good works in heaven means more than it does to those on earth.

"Let it be seen that good works are part of the reason we are having a new world order to live in and live by after the judgment, as all will be part of it in its entirety.

"So all will have to rely on each others good works to live happily and have enough to eat, and to live in harmony and be seen as worthy in my eyes; so do good works whenever you can and whatever you do will be regarded highly by me in my house.

"Let me emphasize that praying for others to step in and help is not regarded as doing good works. You are quite capable of doing the work yourself if you know what is required, and praying for others to do it is not what I want.

"I want you to do the work yourself and that is why you have been told of and made aware of the plights of those in your sight.

"You and you alone will do the good works to alleviate their suffering, not leaving it to your prayers or the prayers of your leaders. Then you will find me in my house ready to embrace you."

"Yahweh, can you explain to the readers how your Son can be sitting in your house in heaven, and at the same time be alive and living on earth, preparing himself to reappear to the masses?"

"Thank you for mentioning this seeming disparity and contradiction of my word that gives the impression that my son is living in heaven and on earth at the same time, Lee.

"No living body resides in any of my houses as it is not possible for a human body to survive in these dimensions. My Son often resides on earth in a human body, and he is to be here to begin his reign on earth when I give him the signal to begin. My son has the ability to communicate with me in my house at any time from anywhere on earth, as you are able to do. When my Son lives on earth his soul has the inclination to come home to visit me often, and he does so."

"You, as a living human have experienced my power to take you out of your physical body and bring you to sit with me and the other elders to take instruction from me. And your body remained behind on earth while you attended a conference here in my presence.

"And you took your time and took the oath, and took the power of telepathic communication and took the power of healing, and took the gift of everlasting life to keep forever, in my house. And you have the power that is in my hand to tell others that life is lived in body and in mind together, and can be separated at will.

"Thank you for explaining and clarifying that, Yahweh."

NEW LAWS

"I am your heavenly Father and this is the only way I am able to tell you what I require from you. And if you are not going to listen to me, then you will not enter my house.

"All of you who have committed crime [sinned] and have been punished by man will also be punished by me.

"All of you who have committed crime and have been punished by man and have asked me to forgive you will be forgiven.

"Any who has murdered and been charged in a court of law and served a sentence, will still have to pay my penalty.

"Any who has murdered and been found guilty in a court of law and has begged my forgiveness, will be forgiven and must also be forgiven by the person they have murdered before entering my house known as the Level of Introduction, in heaven.

"And all those people who have told lies about another, creating harm will have to bear the suffering that the victim suffered.

"All who have caused bodily harm to another will suffer the pain that they inflicted themselves, and they will also be punished.

"Any person who has robbed another will have to pay for this with time in the abyss.

"Any person who has brought grief to another creating emotional upset will feel that emotion and suffer the pain.

"Any person not giving to the poor will have to be poor and they will be poor spiritually, not entering any of my houses and they will remain in hell until I have seen they are sorry.

"Those who think that killing birds and animals is not a crime in my eyes will be punished, as it is a crime. I love the birds and I love all of my creatures, so if you kill them I will punish you!

"All the people who think I am not aware of what they have done are going to be in for a rude awakening as all is kept here and all is recorded for the Day of Judgment. And this record has all of their past lives recorded as well. And even they who are only aware of their present life will have to learn what they did in their previous lives too.

"All those who have committed a crime that did not involve others directly but caused serious problems for the community will also be punished.

"All acts of malice and jealousy will be redirected to the source and this is to be the punishment, and all who have been obsessed with hurting others emotionally will feel this tenfold.

"The ones who have been left in hell and favorably reviewed will be let into a level of light but will not be allowed to enter the heavens as angels, and this is to be their perpetual punishment.

"And all those in hell who have not met the minimum requirements will eventually be extinguished in the abyss.

"The ones who are left to perish will not be allowed to see their loved ones again, and this is final.

"I will supervise the last days and I will supervise the resurrection, and all of my angels and all of my messengers will be doing my work.

"And it will take a thousand years to accomplish and restore the earth to my way. And it will take a thousand years to fix, and it will take a thousand years to right all of the wrongs that bad people have done to my earth.

"And it will be my pleasure to punish them as it is part of me to exact vengeance against those who have destroyed what I have created.

"And if you think that I am easily swayed and that I have a heart of gold that will melt when you cry to be forgiven, then you have not been listening!

"Let it be known to all that the planet earth is to be looked after with loving care, and it is to be washed with a cloth and brushed with a brush and combed with a comb.

"And I mean to be grooming it constantly, bringing a glow to its cheeks and letting it flourish as it was supposed to flourish, and it is to be restored to its former glory.

"And all weapons of war will be discarded. And this is a big job as they have been made by the millions in the USA. And this arsenal is huge and this arsenal will be dismantled and destroyed.

"And all deadly weapons will be taken into safe custody by my messengers and be made into useful items. And these weapons will supply the materials for making useful implements and articles that bring life, rather than death to people.

"The people must realize that I am going to be the one who gives them the opportunity to have this everlasting life. And if they do, they will be with me in one of my houses forever and ever, and if they do not, they will be extinguished.

"I want as many of my children with me as possible as I love them dearly. They are my children and I was responsible for creating all of them; and if you feel that you are better than your neighbor it is only because I have given you this opportunity.

"And if you feel smarter than the man across the road it is only because I have blessed you. And if you are not very intelligent it does not mean that I do not love you as much, just that in this life it is your turn and next time it will be their turn; so be prepared to help each other and be prepared to give selflessly and give help when asked to do so, and also be able to provide assistance to anybody who asks.

"And always be courteous to your elders and be polite to all who speak to you as your thoughts are all recorded. And your thoughts are all in the Book of Records and are here to be read by my angels and messengers.

"And if you possess the ability to travel during your meditations, you may also glimpse the records as some are quite capable of doing this. So be careful in what you do and what you say and what you think, as I know, and if I do not like it, it will reflect on you and my attitude toward you will diminish, along with my love.

"Lee is doing all of this work freely and without complaint as he is a messenger of mine. And in the last days if you are told by one of your spirit guides that you are a messenger of mine, you may want to contact him and tell him, so that he knows who you are.

"He can find you if he asks me but the task will take an enormous amount of time for him. So when judgment time arrives, please tell him if you are one of the chosen messengers and he will be able to give you more details and tell you of my plans, so that you can carry out my work.

"Let it be known that my work will commence soon and my plans will swing into action shortly. My world will be one of turmoil so you must be careful too.

"The world leaders will wage war on each other and this is to be the start of the last days, and you will become aware of them. And during the fighting and killing I will let all my faithful know that I am here, and that I am going to bring an end to it all.

"And the world will stop fighting as I will have it stopped, and the world leaders will be asked to see me. My messengers will escort them to me and I will pass judgment as I have this in mind to rid the world of the evil at the top of the pile first, and shovel the rest from the roadway at ground level. And this is where the pile will be widest and it will be easier for me to do it from there.

"The world must be saved from further destruction and this war will create further problems that will take many years to recover from, and the ecology will be harmed as will all wildlife.

"And the fish in the rivers will die and the bears and the deer will die, and the world will be in grief; and I will become angry with all of you when this starts.

"And my wrath will be felt all over the world so that all will tremble and all will be frightened, and all will scream out for help and all will become frantic; but fear not as my angels will provide safe conduct for you and the others that I want to save.

"And even if you are killed and even if you are living in fear and are hurt, your life will be better than if you are a world leader in these last days, as they are all going to be taken to task and all will suffer greatly, before they perish.

"And I promise the ones who do my work and follow my word that of all people, they will be the winners in this; and of all people they will be my chosen ones, and it will be seen by all people that they are my chosen ones.

"And all who have been saved will wonder at this as they will consider themselves very fortunate, as none really, are the angels they make themselves out to be. So if you are still here at the time and wonder at it, then consider just how wicked and evil were they who did not make it.

"If you are in any doubt as to your status when you arrive, then I will let it be known to you that you are legitimately here and it is not a cruel joke. And I will be looking after you and I will love you, and I will provide for your needs as I did for the Hebrew people when Moses led them through the wilderness for forty years. And this is to be a similar time, as those who are led out will find.

"Let it be known to all that it is to be a time of great joy as well as a time of tribulation. And it will end in victory for the faithful and my love will abound, and it will be spread over the remaining few.

"And let it be known that if you are not a Jew and you are not white that it does not matter as my beloved children are from all religions and races from all over the world.

"And some are more advanced than others but in my eyes all are equal as it is only a matter of time that makes one more skilled than the other. And all will be schooled in many skills by my messengers and all will learn a lot of new skills, and a lot will discard skills no longer needed.

"I have seen many wicked things happen in the past that you would balk at. And if you lived then and were part of it you will be reminded, but for those who were not it is worthwhile noting that this is a part of your historical background, and the lives lost in those skirmishes were lost for nothing.

"And the lives lost in battles waged over lands that are all settled now were all for naught as it is going to be free settlement for any who wish to settle, and those remaining can make the largest house or the smallest cabin their home.

"And all the remaining houses will be removed over time. And all the forests will be regenerated, and all the trees will grow once more, and all of the roadways will be left to grow over and all the rivers and lakes will have fish. And they will have birds and all manner of life living in them, and the world will have an abundance of all living creatures.

"And all that was lost will be restored and all the people left will rejoice in this. And they will love this planet of theirs more than ever before, and they will make it a beautiful paradise as it was meant to be, and this was always my plan, and now my plans are going to be realized.

"I want all of you who are able to, to congregate at your place of worship and pray to me personally to save you. And all those who do this will be given preference in my system, and I will look out for you in the last days and watch over you.

"The last days are going to be horrific as the world will be unleashing atomic terror, and there will be fighting everywhere. And the wicked will be in control of the earth and this is only what is to be expected.

"And the weather will be in accordance with the times and the times are to be turbulent, so be warned and be on your guard against all, as all will be out for themselves and selfishness is to be the main prevalence.

"And your friend will not put his hand out to you and will turn away from you and tell you he does not know you. And the wicked will be on the march and the meek and humble will be in hiding from them.

"And those last days will be remembered for all time as all mankind will go insane and nothing will stop the madness, and nothing will stop the insanity and nothing will save them either.

"Then peace will reign over the world and the only harshness will be the cries of the unholy being led to their deaths, and they will be screaming for mercy like all cowards do.

"And they will be begging to be forgiven as you may well imagine; but did they think of you when they were crucifying you? And did they care about you when you had no bread to eat? And did they stop to help you when you were lost and had nowhere to sleep?

"The refugees known as the Tampa boat people and their children, left on the open boat decking for a week, never knew their fate then, and so you too will not know your fate.

"And I will let you swing in the breeze and let you agonize over this! And I will let you feel the suffering and the pain of these desperate people as they are also my children! And I created them, as well as you!

"And they were the ones who needed your help when you put your hand out and fed them, and you clothed them and gave them a blanket and soothed their fears, and looked after their children.

"And you gave them hope as I give you hope for a better life and this is the reward you are getting, in accordance with the way you treated them!

"All those worthy of entering my house will see wonders unseen before, and the wonders of the world are insignificant compared to the wonders in my house, and if you see one it will amaze you. So imagine the result of seeing all of them, and you will if you are worthy to be in my house as one of my beloved children.

"And you are to be given all that your heart desires, and your rewards are untold as no amount of telling you can describe the joy, and the excitement and euphoria that will be yours.

"And no amount of talking can be adequate when it comes to describing my house as it was built by my own hand, and it is a cathedral comparable to the size of a large city.

"And it is awesome to say the least and it is magnificent to say more. And it is my joy and it is my own palace, and it is where I love to be. And I am sitting in my Cathedral often and I love it.

"You too are invited to sit with me, and you are invited to be seated with the other guests in my house; and I want you to be here as you are part of my family.

"You are part of the universe and I am also part of the universe, so why can we not enjoy the company of each other here in my palace, and why can we not communicate freely with each other here and enjoy each other's company?

"Let it be known that you are one of my children, so tell your friends that you are going to be invited to sit in my house with me. And you are going to be listening to me when you are here and I will be listening to you and your friends.

"Tell your family and your friends that you believe you are going to be speaking to me soon and let them know that they too are going to be able to speak to me with you at the same time. And tell them that they are important in my eyes as I have invited them in as honored guests.

"Remember that I love you and to abide by me and my rules. And you will find me waiting patiently here for you to arrive in paradise."

RELIGIOUS ISSUES

"Yahweh, I want to ask you about some basic religious issues people have been talking about.

"Roman Catholic priests and nuns are not supposed to have sexual intercourse and are told to abstain. This is dreadfully hard for many of them, especially the males, due to males having a much higher libido than females. Is this your wish?"

"Lee, tell all that it is an abomination in my eyes to refuse one of my most precious gifts! And this is to be addressed at the time of judgment!

"And all will have to justify this and explain to me why they have refused to partake of this, my most wondrous gift!

"And this is a slap in my face to turn away from my gift! And they will be punished for this as it has hurt my feelings! And it is a sin in my eyes to do this!"

"But Yahweh, they have been ordered to do this and probably think it is what you expect them to do for you, to grow spiritually."

"Do they think this is what I gave them sexual organs for? And if so why do they use other less important organs, and why do they see and hear?

"Could they not pluck out their eyes and block up their ears instead of refusing this, the most precious gift that I can give my children, the right to procreate from each other and have pleasure from this?

"And why do some say they do not partake of sex publicly then see that sex in private is alright for them? And some of them participate in various sexual deviations, knowing full well that they are sinning.

"So why does the Church not stop this nonsense and allow them to marry and have children as I always intended it to be?"

"Yahweh, what various sexual deviations are they performing?"

"Lee, some have sex with underage children and they participate in ceremonies and have many weird rituals that are unholy. And for centuries they have participated in group sex and orgies that have so many perversions, I cannot bring myself to write them all down.

"So you see it is better for them to acknowledge their sexuality and to take a partner and have children, rather than go to the other end of the spectrum and perform psychosexual deviations behind the front door of the Church.

"All throughout history man has been representing me from his pulpit, and all throughout history these deviations have been prevalent and have been covered up by church members who participate in these abominable activities; and all that are in it shall be exposed by me at the time of judgment."

"Yahweh, are you telling me that the Church has been a hotbed of fornication and sin?"

"Yes, that is exactly what I am telling you and all who read this."

"Yahweh, the perpetrators will explain it away by saying I am doing the devils work, by writing this!"

"Lee, whatever they say in response, nothing can save them from this exposure as I am going to bring them to me and speak to them personally. And they cannot run and hide from me at the time of judgment. So you see they will not be able to refute my word then and if they do it will be more punishment for them."

"Well, it will upset many who read this Yahweh; are you sure you want me to put this in your book?"

"Please place it in my book as all will be written in my name, not your name, and all will tremble at this exposure and all will know my wrath at the time I meet them to dish out my punishment.

"Let all who read this understand that the Church over its entirety is much purer in thought, word and deed than the general populace which has a much lower moral standard of sexual conduct. And any who think that the Church is full of sinners had better start looking at their own lives and the lives of their neighbors as well.

"It will be a time of great tribulation and the people are going to be seen exactly for what they are."

"Yahweh, if sex offenders in the Church are going to be punished for similar types of crime, their exposure will lose impact as few will take much notice, especially if they have also been doing the same sort of thing and are all judged guilty as well."

"Lee, it will be in front of all the angels and all the people will witness each judgment. And this will humiliate them as they will find out what the word shame means, and they will feel great shame too before their punishment."

"Yahweh, this new generation of up and coming theologians are of a higher caliber than their predecessors aren't they?"

"Theology students worldwide generally have little idea of why they are studying except to receive an education. They want to go overseas with the missions and have very big ideas about this though they have very little idea about how this will happen, but will find out. And if they are worthy I will show them how to help and I will show them how to do this too."

"Yahweh, are you responsible for all the murders in society by turning a blind eye to them, allowing wicked people to kill others?"

"If you think I can be a God of mercy then I will be, and if you think I can be a God of justice then I will be; and if you think I can be a God of kindness then I will also be.

"But if you think I am a God who kills people and a God who creates trouble, then you have not heard about me from my own mouth and you have heard about me from another source!

"And my works are for the salvation of, and not the destruction of mankind.

"It is imperative you show the people this and I am going to be here for the duration as you are. And all who perish will never be seen or heard of again and all who remain will live on forever.

"So be astute, and do not include any that are unworthy of you and me, and I am going to see if they are worthy or not. And if you mistake some I will find out and remove them from my house as you are to learn to find out all of their details, as you are capable.

"You are astute and none can deceive you and none can lie to you as you can see through them, and none can be cleverer than you because they are not, as I instruct you, and none can be your master as you are their master and they are your servant.

"Be frank with them and tell them straight who you are and what your role is and who they are and what their role is. And be quite firm and be very, very adamant in your decisions and I will verify them. And I will pass them back to you if you have made any mistakes.

"Be prudent and see if I will allow them into my house or not and remember the rules as you have been told, and remember what I want, and remember what you want too.

"Be truthful and open and honest with them and they will be alright as long as they realize you are also in judgment of them, and you are my messenger, doing this for me.

"It is sad that people are killing each other to see if they can have power over each other. And I have been saddened today thinking about the people who are to die shortly as I know who they are. And I am really very upset at this and wish I could stop it, and I will, one day.

"But for now it must express itself as it has been determined and I would like you to say a few words for me in the next weeks about the way life is deteriorating for all of us. And the world is heading into a war far more terrible than any that went before.

"If the politicians are truthful they will agree and if the people are clever they will see but I doubt if this will happen as you know already the people are limited intellectually, and you know already that most politicians are outrageous liars."

"Yahweh, tell me… why have you made the people so limited intellectually?"

"Lee, if the people had more intellect the rate of crime would soar and the rate of detection would decrease as they would outsmart the law, and they would be far smarter than the authorities. And they would be far cleverer than the politicians, and the world would be run by criminals, and the world would be full of violence, and the world would be full of corruption.

"Is it not far better to have it as it is with the people in blissful ignorance rather than be fully aware of all that is happening? And is it not far better to have the people in a state of ignorant bliss rather than make them face the harsh realities that so few are aware of, and even less are able to see or comprehend?

"It is imperative that people are kept to a level of intelligence that is able to sustain them and not overwhelm them. And it is imperative that the people are told only what they need to know as reality is too difficult for them to grasp. And it must be this way as otherwise it would be too hard for them to live in harmony with each other.

"If people were too intelligent it would be one trying to outdo the other and trying to take advantage of those with less. And they do this now in a big way; so imagine if they had even more ways of working out how to rob the elderly and disadvantaged of their possessions and pensions, and their little bit of money.

"If you have more than your neighbor, it creates envy and if you have less than your neighbor it creates a distinction between you. So is it not better that we who are in the spirit world have no possessions and have nothing to covet, and nothing is needed at all?

"It will be like that on earth after the judgment as no-one need buy anything as all will be provided for by the neighbor. And if they need food they will grow it, and if they need a house they will have one to suit them. And if they need any sort of thing to make life easier then it will be made available to them by the messengers.

"None will be sick and none will be lonely and none will ever hunger or thirst. And none will be idle as all will be fit and healthy and want to be active, working the fields or tending their flock.

"It will be a time of great joy and anyone who wants to live in my house can, and anyone who wants to share in the joys of the earth can. So it will be a joy to be in either place and it will be a joy to be here to share in it, and a joy to be aware of all things as people will learn many more things if they live forever, and do not die.

"It is not my wish to condemn the Jehovah's Witnesses by belittling their ideas and it is not my wish to belittle the Catholic Church by bringing attention to their practices, but these following issues must be addressed as soon as is possible.

"I decree it unholy to drink the blood of any! The cup of wine at the Last Supper was taken to be the blood of my Son and this is a symbol of love for his sacrifice. It is not my wish to have people drink blood.

"This is the proper time and place to say it here and I will make it quite clear that the practice of taking bread and wine is alright only if it is taken symbolically in memory of my Son. Transubstantiation is a thought that grew and has been a thorn in my side for centuries.

"Get rid of this nonsense and take the Communion as a way to express your love for my Son, not as a way to humiliate me by pretending I am working needless miracles.

"The taking of medicine is not the same as drinking blood. Some medicines have been made with the blood of men and women and these save lives.

"The practice of transfusing blood from one to another gives an opportunity to live as it is this that keeps the heart pumping. And it is good as otherwise the heart would stop and that is not my intention. I gave you life to live, not to be shortened, and if your life can be saved by taking a donation of blood then it is in my best interest too, as I created life to live, not to die.

"And I created life to enjoy, not to be in fright and not to live in fear, so it is my wish that all are aware that this donating of blood is acceptable in my eyes, and I would not frown on anyone who receives this life saving donation from another. And this is my final word on that subject.

"Tell all who listen that the practice of homosexuality is not unholy as it is my wish that men and women can love whomever they desire. And it is the promiscuity that angers me, not love as love is me and I am love so why would I not be happy to see love?

"Tell all those who listen that they are all my children and I love them as much as they would love their own children. I love them and it is not my intention to deny them the chance of finding happiness, and it is not my intention for the church [as an established hierarchy] to deny them access to me by bigotry and misinformation.

"And I would not want any to feel that they are unable to speak to me, and they are not to be forgotten, and they are to be told this.

"Tell any who listens to my word that I am here for all of my children and I will always be here for my children, and I love all of them equally. So why would I not love one who desires another of the same sex, as this is an expression of love too.

"Tell them that I have an undying love and that my love is forever and that I will not deny anyone who comes to me and accepts my Son as their Savior. And tell anyone who listens to me and reads about me that I am here to give them a gift even greater than they could ever imagine.

"Tell all of them this and tell all of them over and over so they know. And tell them many times over so that it sinks in, and tell them many times over until they get the message.

"Tell me who is listening to my word and tell me who is not listening so I can deliver my word to them personally, and I will. And no-one will be left in any doubt that I can do this as I can, and I am going to do it and it will be done!

"Let all who listen understand my wishes and let all who listen be here to listen, not working in the field on the Sabbath as it is hard to tell those who are busy exactly what my plans are.

"And it is my wish that they congregate to hear my preaching on one day of the week, as I want all to know my plans for them.

"And as they are coming to a time when judgment is around the corner it is now imperative they come into my house of worship and listen to my word, and they are to take heart from this.

"Tell all who will listen about my plans. And they will rejoice as it is written and prophesized. And it has been told over and over to each generation for two thousand years now and if it has not been heard by now, it will be heard before the last day.

"And I promise that none will be here standing before me without prior warning, and if they have refused to listen then it is their own doing, not my doing.

"And even though I love them they have not loved me. So what can I do but turn them away from me and say to them, 'You have not shown me loyalty and you have not shown me that you love me, and look what I have given you!'

"This is what I will tell them and if they respond that they are now convinced, it will be too late as they were told yesterday and it is today I am judging them; and it is today I make my decision about them, so be told and listen, as it is important for you to hear me.

"And it is important to take heed of me and it is important that you are saved. And it is important that you are taken into my house as I want you and I love you. And if you turn away from me it will sadden me greatly. So please ask me to forgive you of your sins and your bad ways, and I will. And if you do not believe this then forget it, as I will forget you too!

"Tell them that it is a long time to stay in hell if they have been placed there and it is a long time to waste as it could be productive. And they are going to be able to see and hear in heaven whereas those in hell do not see and do not hear anything, as it is my punishment for them.

"And only those who are in my houses can see and only those with me in my houses can hear. And those who can see and hear are my children with me, and those who cannot see and hear are in the house of Satan.

"And it is there they will stay until my final judgment of them and will wish it was not on their heads. And they will wish they had listened; but they thought they knew better than all of the others, and heeded nothing.

"Tell them that this is all avoidable by asking me to forgive them now. They only need to ask and it will be done. And if they ask me personally it will be better as I will know it was from them and not from another, asking me to forgive them.

"My love for them will grow and my heart will melt and my happiness will overflow and my joy will be abundant. And my life will be worthwhile, as my children will have come to me and asked me to forgive them, and I will.

"Let all who come into my house be here for me and for their own reasons, and let all who do not wish to be in my house for any reason, remain outside.

"Love is not all that counts in life and some have not had love and some have had more than their fair share. I love all of my children equally and I will give them plenty to share.

"And all will bask in my love and all will enjoy being loved as I am their loving Father and I will show them my love.

"I will show them how much I love them by giving them gifts that are forever and will remain forever, and this is to be their reward.

"Let all who love me have these rewards and let all who deny me have rewards of a different nature. Let those who seek me have me and those who seek Satan have Satan, and those who do not care about me or about Satan, will find him anyway!

"Let my people love each other in the world and let those in spirit love each other too, as why should they not love each other because they are in spirit and not in body?

"Let all have the capacity to love and let all have the capacity to share the joys and the emotions that we share with our loved ones daily. It will not change and we will remember how much it means to us to give our love to our families and our friends, and this will remain the same.

"Let any who ask have love and any who ask have friendship and any who ask have companionship, and all will be with their families and all will have friends. And all will find a happiness that is not known yet, and all will have the most emotional and most uplifting experience in their existence, once they have entered my house.

"And my house is large and my house is warm and my house is full of good things. And my house is going to be your house and the rent is free. And there is no charge at all as you are my honored guest. And my children are always invited into my home as guests, and this home will then be your home.

"My Son is waiting with his arms outstretched to embrace you and he will. My Son will be ready to receive you into his heart and his home. My Son is my seat on which I sit in my house and he holds the Kingdom of God in his hand as he is the trustee.

"My Son wants you here to enjoy his company in my presence, and he will ask you to join him in his endeavors too. My wish is that you embrace him and take what he and I have both offered you, freely.

"Our offer will not expire and you are to see that it is forever, not to be taken lightly or amicably with frivolity, but taken in full seriousness with thought to your future. And that is why it is so important that you take time to go to your local house of worship and pray that I let you into my house.

"Remember to ask me for everlasting life as well, as you will be here for a long time, and time has no limits in my house. My love for you grows by the day and I want you to be home with me to enjoy what is here, ready and prepared for you."

THE PLAN

"Let us begin this by letting all know that the end is not the end and that my plans are for all of mankind and not 144,000 as told by one religion.

"This is a number given in the Bible to show how many helpers there are going to be and these helpers are people who live and have lived on earth and will help my Son and the nine houses of angels carry out my plans at the time of judgment and thereafter.

"It is going to be a hectic time when the Messiah arrives as he will come when the judgment is apparent and not before then. My Son will arrive from afar and will be seen to appear. And he will arrive with many other messengers who will be accompanying him.

"The sun will have not risen and he will appear when it is starting to shine once more. My Son will instruct those he meets and his instructions will be carried out. I am the one who wants these things carried out, not my Son who is going to speak on my behalf.

"Let all who hear his words heed him and let all who heed him be my helpers. Let all who do not heed him be taken prisoner, bound hand and foot and brought before me to show me why they are so defiant!

"Let any who dare defy me be taken away and shackled in chains as many will want their blood and many will be angry with them! And my Son will remove their many demons and try to save them.

"Let the people clamor for my Son and let them ask him questions about the resurrection and the last days and the judgment and Armageddon!

"Let any who seek his help have it and let any who want to hold his hand, do so.

"And any who try to harm my Son will perish, and I mean it!

"Let all who ask him to be healed, be well, and let all who have multiple medical problems be restored!

"Let all who ask for help in any way receive help and any that need help will get it!

"It is going to be a wonderful occasion and it is going to be free of all fighting, and free of all rioting and free of all of those wicked things!

"Let it be known that I am returning to be on earth with my Son and that my life will be one of resting with you on earth, in my temple. It will be a time for great celebration too as the war will come to an end and the ones responsible will be called to task, then cast out.

"Let any leader who has been involved with the running of a corrupt and warring government be warned; they will certainly perish, unless forgiven.

"And there has been a shocking war of terror; and the king of terror appeared from within the bushes; and lo, from among the bushes sprang forth the king of terror.

"Let it be known that my Son himself will speak to the king of terror and subdue him shortly before I judge him and punish him.

"Let all know that his life as the king of terror is finished, and he will spend time in hell suffering unending agonies, before he perishes.

"Let any who think I am jesting feel this agony and any who have actively supported this terrorist will suffer the same consequences, as without your support, the king of terror could not have reigned.

"Let any who feel that they can pray to me and be forgiven for this terror find out the truth. And that is, they will be forsaken and lost and they will not have any chance of being saved at all.

"Any who disagree with my judgment can call upon my Son and ask him to review their sentence, but woe-betide anyone who does this without just cause as I am a kind and loving Father and my judgments are sound.

"So be warned, any who cry out for mercy and any who ask for clemency and are guilty as charged will be punished even more than they thought possible.

"And it will be a long term of punishment and it will be an agonizing punishment, and I mean agonizing. And my words will live up to their expectations, and they are meant to.

"Let any who read this and find humor, be the subject of my wrath and it will be a harsh and cruel punishment as I am a harsh and cruel God if I want to be. And if you do not believe this, look about you and see how the animals of the prairie and the animals of the jungle live, and see that they kill each other and eat each other!

"And if you find kindness in this let me know as you must have a heart like mine. And if you have a heart like mine then you will tremble in fear as my wrath is going to be shown to you, and my love is not going to be seen at all. So be warned that my will is my way and my wrath is my pleasure as your wrath is your pleasure!

"Let all understand that my wrath is the wrath of justice and not of the same ilk as the war lords who create war for control and power over the weaker nations.

"My Son will be looking at it all in his own way and he will administer justice to those who have broken my Commandments. And his judgments will be like your judgments, hard and uncompromising, as your heart is like rock and your mind is set like concrete and cannot be changed.

"My Son will tell all of you that my life has been one of unswerving kindness and of total loyalty to you, and has not interfered in your daily life.

"I keep my distance, observing from afar and I have everything written down. My angels keep all of the records here for you to look at, and even your first breath is recorded as well as your last.

"Let it be known now that most of you have been helped by my angels though some have not. My angels help any that call for assistance and pray to me, who then sends them to assist you.

"Let it be known that most of you have been in trouble at one time or another and that I have taken pity on you, and my angels have given you their assistance, unbeknownst to you.

"Let it also be known now that my life is in devotion to my children and I watch over you in your daily life as well as create new life. My life is one of creating and the people are aware that they share the earth with other creatures of my making.

"All creatures are my creations and this is to give the earth an abundance of life, and to have many species that help each other to live, though most are in the food chain of life, and this is unavoidable for the survival of all.

"My creations are my joy and this gives me my greatest pleasure as I watch them and enjoy their lives with them. All creatures are precious to me and my plans though strange to you, are not to me.

"And my way is strange to you but not to me, so do not ask me why they eat each other and why they kill their own offspring, and why they kill their own in times of famine and in times of danger.

"Let all know that the plans have been looked at with an eye to improving life and this is to happen after the Day of Judgment.

"The animals will have far more to eat in this time than before and the food they eat will be provided for by me, and I will nurture them. I will provide for them as I provided for my children in the desert for many years, bringing food to them daily.

"Let no-one feel threatened by me or my Son unless they have a specific reason to be and if you have a reason, speak now and tell me so that we can reconcile before it is too late.

"My Son will be here and he is to speak to all of you, and if you ask him to forgive you he will, as he is my servant and he will do this for me as well as for you.

"Let any who feel that they have sinned and cannot be forgiven speak up as it is my plan to save you, and this is why you must say what you have done and admit it to me or to my Son, and then you will be saved and not face certain death.

"Let any who are forgiven and saved from certain death know that a punishment is awaiting them as they must atone for their sin.

"Let any who think they are unable to be saved also say their piece as all who come to me to be forgiven, will be forgiven.

"Let any who criticize my Son be aware that he is the one they must ask to be allowed into my house, as he holds the key.

"No-one else can open the door to my house except my Son, so be wary of who you speak to and be careful not to insult him.

"Play with fire rather than play with words when speaking to him as your future wellbeing is in your own hands, not his, and he is here to persuade you to come into my house, not turn you away.

"Let my Son tell you himself that you are a child of mine. You have every right to come into my house and you have every right to be here. I have given you a name at birth and this is what I will call you, as it is the name I have given you, not the name your parents on earth gave you.

"And my Son will tell them that they are all going to be asked for an explanation as to why they have been giving me a bad time and why they have only spoken my name in vain, and why they have not spoken to me and why they have been bad to me, and why they speak to Satan, and not to me.

"And why is it that they find it easier to say my name in anger and disappointment than in enlightenment and in love? This annoys me as I am their loving Father, not one who gives them trouble; so please tell them that this is to stop as I get offended with it, and it hurts my feelings, and I cry out in frustration over this!

"Tell them my feelings are easily hurt and I am consoled by no-one, but they are consoled by others and can be comforted.

"It has a long-lasting effect on my happiness to be called by my name in vain. And it hurts me to think I have impressed them so little they curse with my name and the name of my Son who died on the Cross, to show them that they are to have everlasting life if they believe in him, and then they say that this is a fiction!

"Let all who believe say so now and all who do not believe tell me now so that I can write your name on the scroll and it will be read out at the time of judgment.

"Let any who think that judgment time will be a time of milk and honey be seen in my house as a fool. And it will be a harsh time, not the wonderful chitchat that you have in the marketplace and not the lovely afternoon tea spent with your maiden aunt in the comfort of her own home.

"And it will not be a time of shouting out in the streets about how wonderful life is, as all will be subdued and all will feel frightened as the sun will not shine for three days, and then all will be glorious once more.

"Let it then be apparent who is here and who is missing as all will try to find their loved ones.

"Let it be apparent that those missing are being punished and some will perish!

"Let it be apparent that those suffering in hell for their crimes will either perish, or be allowed into heaven when my anger with them has subsided.

"Let it be known that these people as spirits will be allowed into a level of light apart from the others, as they will not be allowed to enjoy the privileges that are provided for the pure of heart.

"Let it be known that the pure of heart will be in my house with me immediately after judgment, not left in the Level of Higher Learning waiting to enter, but invited in as soon as they have been judged.

"Let all be aware that once in my house with me they are to be given gifts and are to be given many wonderful things.

"And any who feel they can tell me about the past and are unhappy with their future find my wrath. And it will be a sorry day for them, as I will tell them they are to leave and join the others who are outside the door.

"Many will want to see their relatives who remain outside and if it is my will, this can be done.

"Let all know that life in heaven is better than life on earth and my rules are lenient and no-one will find fault with their neighbor.

"It is to be a wonderful life, like the times when the sun shone brightly, the crops were bountiful and food was plentiful.

"The levels of light will be replaced with a level of happiness and all who are in the higher levels will find more happiness.

"My plan is to allow all of you to find happiness at the higher levels, so it is your choice as to whether or not you join this plan, to gain a better place in one of the houses.

"And all who are higher will be closer to me, your heavenly Father. So if you love me dearly, then I will love you dearly, and you will be closer to me than your neighbor.

"My future plans include you as you will find out, and you will have the opportunity to join in and help me with these.

"Let it happen that the planets will eventually be filled and teeming with all manner of life as is found on earth.

"Let it happen that new types of life are created and these are nurtured and looked after.

"Let it happen that my angels will look after this new life and you will help create it too.

"Let all know that my plans for you are not mandatory and if you choose another path, feel free to follow it to fulfill your own dreams.

"Let my plans be open for all to enjoy and let all be part of them.

"My children are my joy and were my plan and now my plan will be fulfilled shortly and my plan has been successful to date.

"Let it then be that the plans I have for my children are successful and that they too enjoy creating their own universes as much as I have enjoyed it.

"Let it be that all have autonomy, to do whatever they want to do.

"Let my children share my joy of creating new life, and sharing in the responsibility that is forthcoming, and let all have a say in matters pertaining to doing this for themselves, if they want this.

"Let it happen that my plans are complete and that my children have more knowledge and more power, and that they are made in my image and that they are my successors.

"Let all know this is possible and that with time you will become what I am now, as you are made in my image.

"Let it be known how you feel about this by telling me and if you do not want this, tell me, and I will take your name off the scroll.

"Let it happen that you have the opportunity to be part of this plan, and if you follow your own path then you have my blessings too.

"My children's happiness is my only concern, therefore if you feel unhappy with this let me know now, and I will find out what is causing your unhappiness, and rectify it.

"Let it be said that I am a loving Father and that my plans for you are a token of my love, and my plans for you have been thought through and I have given you my greatest gift; that is, the gift of everlasting life and never-ending joy.

"Let it be known now that you are to be allowed free reign and no-one will stop you from your plans, as no-one has stopped me. And your joy will overflow as mine will, to see you happy and contented.

"Let it be known that this is why I have put you all to a test of strength, and a test of character.

"And I have given you many trials and tribulations to strengthen your capacity to get things accomplished, not sitting down by the roadside watching the labors of others and doing nothing yourself.

"Let me tell you that the emotional pain you felt when death took the ones you loved away will be replaced with a joy untold and unknown.

"And this too is my reward and this is true, and this is for you and is a token of my love.

"Let all know that other life is abundant in the universe and that all saved souls will discover this, whether on earth or in heaven.

"Let it become known that these other beings are also my children as I created them as well as you, and they are part of my plan too.

"Let it happen that you are kind and loving to all of my creations everywhere, the same as you will be to all those you create, and you will know the joy of loving your own creations too.

"Make it happen that all other beings are aware of you and you are aware of them, and you are there to help them whenever they ask.

"Let me tell you some beings are similar to you and have advanced further than you have, though most are far less advanced.

"Let all who have this in writing tell me they will do this as it is important to me that all of my children are cared for, and they will be as happy as you will be.

"Let it be known that my children are not all people like you and are not all seen by you, and that there are other dimensions that are a mystery to you, and may always be so.

"My plans include all of those beings too and you are part of this, so be aware that this is so and do not interfere with their progress.

"Let it happen that they are to evolve at their own rate of evolution, and even though you may see many things not good in your eyes, keep it in mind that they are my children and I will look after them.

"Let me say that my creations will be still evolving for millions of years until they are ready to know you.

"My children have many forms and you will find many of them, so be aware of this and you will be left alone too, as they wish to be.

"My diligent angels are always here to help you in heaven and when you enter my house you will meet many of them. And you will find many are very old and wise and you will find many have been helping me with my creations, and this is what they have been doing.

"Let it be known that you are to be an angel in my house, and you are to take a prominent position alongside those who have been here since the beginning.

"Let it also be known that my angels are your friends and they are here for you and you will be their equal too.

"Let all have the stored knowledge of all your past lives, and the knowledge will be enormous as all will be restored in your memory to have once more.

"Let all remember all you ever did and all you ever thought about and all that ever happened to you, so you can learn from this and grow from this and utilize this knowledge, and remember who you knew before and who was a family member and who was a friend.

"Be aware that all your past lives are stored within your higher-self, and when you become spirit again you rejoin your higher-self to become as one, and this is how all your memories will be made available to you once more.

"Be aware that you are your higher-self in part, and each life you have had makes up all of you, and the knowledge is accumulated.

"Be aware that all you have become is the result of many lives and this covers a time-period of many years, depending on the amount of reincarnations you have had.

"Be aware that I have watched each life and each life has been reincarnated from the light, and not reincarnated from any life left on the earth plane.

"Be aware that all souls left on the earth plane are actually in hell's waiting room awaiting judgment. And all are there for a reason and cannot come to the light unless forgiven. And forgiveness is only given by me, by my Son or by my messengers.

"Let it be known that all who are let into the light from the earth plane are in the kingdom of heaven, not in my house, the Kingdom of God, as none are in the Kingdom of God until judgment day and invited in.

"Let it be known that my Son is still able to be with me here and will be here, and you will meet him, and he will be the one to welcome you into our house.

"Let it be known that my Son is still the Son and that you are to be an angel. My Son is from my Holy Spirit, and he is from me and born to the Virgin Mary.

"Let all know that my Son's word is to be heard above the rest and he has authority to do things that you cannot do.

"Let it be known that my Son is my hope for you and he is to be heard above any other, and his word is the same as my word.

"Let all realize that he is the one who died for you and his sacrifice was for all of you. And he did this to prove that he loved me; and he did this for another reason, and that reason was to prove to you that there is life after death! Let my Son give me his time and he will give you his time too!"

MY DESIRES

"It is my desire to convey the following information to all who read this, my word and my last testament, and my desire is to educate those following my pathway so that they may have everlasting life.

"My desire is to let you know that I have the power to give you everlasting life, and I have the power to give you abilities to cope with more than you ever thought possible.

"My desires encompass many concepts unknown to date. And these desires will manifest soon once the judgment has been finalized, so that my children will be able to enjoy their new existence, with me in my house.

"My desires include bringing my children into a new world order. And it includes bringing my children into a way of existing not seen before, and this is to make sure all can be happy in my house.

"My desires are all that are needed as I know the needs of my children because I created them, and I gave them the needs that they have, therefore, all have needs that will be catered for.

"Let it happen that my needs are also fulfilled, and to accomplish this we will be doing my work in the following way:

"Let it be known that my wishes are to give everlasting life to all those sharing my house with me.

"And lasting friendship with each other without disharmony.

"Long term goals that can be accomplished by those undertaking them.

"A desire to help those on earth who remain to look after it.

"A long term commitment to help clean up the planet earth.

"A sustained effort to become as high as possible in this new order.

"Long term goals which will include creating life on other planets.

"Let it happen then and this is what I would expect of you and I will let you accomplish these goals.

"My Son will help you with any needs that you think you will have and he will answer any questions you may put to him. The new order will have an hierarchy and my Son will delegate duties that are deemed necessary.

"Let it be seen then that I am able to confidently leave you on the way to develop yourself and become independent, so that you are able to have your own thoughts and do your own work, and if you require help with this it will be provided for you."

"Thank you Yahweh, now may I ask you to respond to some very personal questions about your actions or lack thereof, on earth?"

"Let me tell you that all is an open book here Lee, so ask me now while you are in my presence."

"Yahweh, are you guilty of premeditated murder by allowing animals to eat each other, and also by knowing humans are going to murder each other, without making any effort to stop them?"

"Lee, it is a good question and I defend myself profusely.
It is not my hand that strikes and it is not my thought behind the hand!

"The murders that happen cannot usually be stopped. And the murder is for a reason entirely in the mind of the murderer. I do not stop the natural order of events as the earth is mankind's domain.

"My angels will help if called or dispatched or if they are in the vicinity and can intervene in time, by divine intervention.

"Apart from accidents and crime the chain of events is largely predetermined and without this progressive chain of daily events unfolding, the world's progression would not turn out as thought."

"Yahweh, are we living a life that has already been pre-planned to some degree by ourselves?"

"Yes, and it is for you to develop from this during your time in heaven. And it is this predetermined life that is your life now as you predetermined it yourself at the time you were in my light. And this life is the plan you made for yourself.

"It is predetermined so you are able to experience all that is to be. And it is for you to have good as well as bad; and some like to experience all good and some all bad in their lives, so it is all balanced out, as you will find.

"If your life has been one of great suffering and you have had what appears to be astonishingly bad luck, this was pre-planned by you to experience this anxiety. And it is this that will make you stronger later on, and this stress you constantly feel is going to be lifted as it is for a reason, and so all things are for a reason."

"Yahweh, this is confusing as you say all people will be judged for their crimes, and all souls who have committed crimes will be left in spirit on the earth plane, unless forgiven.

"And if people know the lives they have planned for themselves are going to include major crime which leads to the abyss, followed by the second death after judgment, then why would anyone want it?

"Why would anyone put themselves through this or put themselves in this situation if they could avoid it? And why say that humans have free will if all is predetermined and then approved by you?"

"Lee, it is confusing and life is full of contradictions. The reason I let you all predetermine your life is to let you have an input into the planning of your own destiny and to give you control over your life.

"This control however, is limited and is left up to your guides to manage and does not include criminal activity, and all who commit these crimes do so after they have been allowed to reincarnate.

"And these crimes are not part of your predetermined plan as it is apparent that you would have known you were to be punished."

"Yahweh, as your messenger, I speak to deceased people at will and find those who have been murdered are angry and want to avenge their murder, and want the murderer brought to justice.

"Most murder victims refuse to leave the earth plane until their body has been unearthed and the crime is accounted for."

"Yes, Lee, and this is why they do not want to come to the light until it has been resolved, as the perpetrator has committed a crime and this crime must be seen to be paid for, and it will be paid for in my house at the time of judgment.

"Any worthy person who has been murdered will live on earth again as I have explained that reincarnation is a fact. And those who die like this will live again if they desire this, and those worthy souls who die like this will see their loved ones again in heaven.

"The murderer and their victim remain tied to the earth plane until the murder has been resolved in the mind of the victim. And the murderer cannot move on unless this is the case, even if prayed for.

"The victim may stay with the murderer to see the crime is not forgotten and will only move on if asked to by a messenger. If not worthy to enter the light, the victim will remain on the earth plane.

"Those victims worthy of entering the kingdom of heaven may do so at any time, and they have a chance of being judged worthy of entering my house, the Kingdom of God, at the time of judgment.

"Now, let me now tell you some more about the last days, Lee.

"It will now be evident even to the most gullible that the former world leaders were liars and it will become increasingly evident that they were doing things not in the best interest of the people, but in their own best interest, for their own gain.

"To determine this truth, examine your bank balance and then examine their bank balance and you will see plainly and clearly for yourself in whose interest they were working for.

"Let it happen then that they have this pleasure as it is part of the final days. And the end times you know as Armageddon will soon be upon you. And it has already been plotted and planned by unscrupulous leaders to attack and destroy your depleted nations.

"It will be a blood bath until now not ever seen or heard of before. And you will be angry and you will be shocked at the horror, and it will continue until you can barely think straight. And you will be beside yourself with grief at the terror and the loss of life and the waste of all things.

"This is mankind's doing, not my doing and not Satan's doing either, just mankind's way as it is and has been; and it is to be their last pleasure as I will stop it mid-stream and punish all involved.

"Let me say that this war will be upon you all soon Lee, and you must ignore it and not become engrossed in it as your time is near to help judge the wicked, and you will be here with me soon.

"Let it be seen by all reading this that Lee is to help in judging too, as it is the way, and it is my will that this is to be so.

"Let it be seen that Lee will be in my house with me helping in this and that he is to be here with me in these turbulent times. And he is to be seen helping me, and this is the time he is to be here.

"Lee, tell me now if you want this position or not, and if not I will delegate this duty to another if you so wish.

"Let me know if you feel able to do my work, and if not tell me now, and let it be known that my Son is going to be here too, to bring relief from oppression. And he is to bring justice and world peace and order into the world, and the unscrupulous leaders will perish.

"My Son is to take over the supply and administration of the main food supplies and will arrange the transportation and distribution of these, and he will organize most things and will tell all of you what to do.

"And my Son is experiencing some anxiety and anguish as he has been through a very difficult life preparing for this time.

"And he has experienced all of the pain and suffering you have felt already, so be told that he can empathize with you in that he understands your problems and needs; and he will be able to recognize them instantly, bringing relief, not death to you.

"And he will bring medicine to you and freedom to you, not prisons with razor-wire fences, and not bashings and recriminations for being who you are, but love and kindness and compassion as you will see.

"And this will be hard to take too as it has not been seen before by mankind in this day and age, and greed and power has warped the minds of all of you.

"And you have forgotten how to love each other and how to look after each other, and even how to keep each other alive. And you have forgotten how to show kindness to each other and how to give to each other, and how to show compassion for each other.

"And this is to be seen once more as my Son did this many years ago and was crucified by the Romans and Jews for it. And he will be addressing the perpetrators about this, and he will want to ask them many questions.

"Let it be seen that justice will prevail and all things that have been unjust will be taken up and looked at and this will be the beginning of a new age in time, and this time will be the start of my judgment.

"And I will be in charge of all things that happen in this time and no man will have any authority over another as all will be equal, and no man or woman will be looked upon as inferior to another.

"Let me say that all things are to be addressed and those who live in poverty will have my riches and my best food and my warmest bed, and those who lavishly live in luxury will be out in the manger with the animals.

"Let it be seen that those who have indulged in the finest linen and the finest clothing and have the finest of everything I have provided on earth, that it is for a reason, and that reason is, they are to begin retribution for their hedonistic lifestyle. And this life of luxury is a small taste of what they are to leave behind when I extinguish their selfish souls forever.

"And they are to see this is the last time they will enjoy these blessings that I have provided for them, so be told this and be aware that they are to perish soon.

"Let me say one more thing to you, reading this today.

"My wish is that you find me in my house and for you to live in peace and harmony with me here.

"My wish is to have you in my house with my angels rejoicing in a life of luxury, and not agonizing over your past sins.

"Remember to ask me to forgive you and ask me to allow you into my house, and you will be in my heart as well."

THE PURPOSE

The ancient Hebrews had this notion that God is time as they used to say that his name is Yahweh which means 'I Am' as God said to them 'I am and I will be', so the biblical God is the God of time living in 'the now', which is the present, being existentially ever present and omnipresent in the now.

God says he created us from nothing at all. To create us God had to think about us with thought. From this, we came into being from a thought and we exist in no time and no space, which is 'the now.'

To create us then it is obvious that God had to make time and space. Time and space could not have existed before there was nothing at all. If not, is this life 'the now' we perceive we are living in only a thought of God's? Can a thought ever see the one who created it? Can a thought have definable boundaries?

"Yahweh, would you mind spending some of your valuable time with me explaining this?"

"Lee, it is your Father in heaven and I will define this all for you in a way that is understood so it will be rudimentary in its entirety. And If you like you can ask me questions."

"Thank you, Yahweh."

"Yahweh, before you existed, what was there?"

"Lee, there was nothing at all and this is hard to explain to you who are three dimensional and see and feel and look about at all things and say, 'But how is it possible that there was nothing at all?'"

"That is correct Yahweh; you mean when you say nothing at all, that not even the atoms that make up matter, and not even the space for these atoms to be in, existed anywhere, don't you?"

"Yes, that is exactly right, and 'nothing' is very hard to explain to people and without an explanation people cannot work it out."

"Are you going to explain it then, Yahweh?"

"Yes, but it is more than just a few lines as it will take a lot of your time and patience to write all of it down, as it takes more time to write it down than it is, and it is nothing, so the written explanation of nothing is more, and more is hard to explain.

"Let us begin: In the beginning there was nothing and this nothing was not a place or not a thing and not a void.

"This nothing was without substance, had nothing inside it and nothing outside it, and took no space and there was no space.

"It is hard to tell you exactly what became from nothing and it is hard to tell you what was before nothing too."

"Yes Yahweh, it is hard for me to understand what it means that there was nothing at all."

"From nothing, there became something, and from something, there became everything, and this is the secret of the universe, that all that is, is actually nothing!"

"Everything you do is a part of my own thought and everything in this universe is a part of my thought, and all that is in existence is a part of my thought. And that is why I say that I am omnipresent because it is true. And that is why I say that I am in everyone because it is true.

"And I am having difficulty with it as it has become a nightmare for me now that the people are fighting each other continuously over their ill conceived grievances and greed.

"And that is why I am stopping it very soon and that is the reason... that is the reason I want it stopped, as the people who are doing this are creating too many problems for me.

"Each person has developed his or her own unique individuality and has become independent from me, the original thought. All you see and all you do is from your own thoughts so you too create things from thought."

"Yahweh, you say this thought that happened and became you appeared at random from nowhere?"

"Yes, that is what I said and am saying, and the reason is that a thought is from a thought, is from a thought. And original thought without inspiration is virtually impossible, so the reason that I came into being is virtually impossible and the odds are inconceivable."

"Is it possible that there is more than even you are aware of Yahweh? I mean you might be the scientist inside the laboratory but the whole world might be outside the laboratory door."

"Lee, not possible!"

"Why not, Yahweh?"

"It is so! I am the Alpha and the Omega! And the beginning and the end is my plan! And my plan is that you are to be part of the plan! And you are to do my work! And you are to help with this!

"And you are to see to it and you will do this for me, as I am your heavenly Father! And I want to know if you are willing to do this?"

"Yes Yahweh, I am willing to help.

"Yahweh, is there a scientific way to explain nothing and how from nothing there became something and from this something, everything came into being?"

"Yes Lee, I am difficult to understand and you are patient, so I will explain it in other terms now.

"From within an atom there is space and through that space is another void or another dimension. It is a balance between infinity and non-existence. And it is a place and a non-place and it is in the vicinity of itself. And it becomes a huge, infinitesimally small and infinitesimally large, alternating, agitating cosmic continuum and it is at a temperature beyond your measurement as temperature is like time.

"The temperature is like nothing at all as this is a perception of mankind's too, so the nothing is like your emotions that become into being from a thought and the emotion creates the feeling of pain or joy, and this pain is something real to you and this joy is something real to you too.

"And this was nothing before the emotion and this nothing then became something that you yourself created and that is the way of it all.

"And my thoughts create the space you are living in and my thoughts create you who live in the space and my thoughts create the environment that you perceive you live in and this is all from me, and I am the Creator."

"Where did this first atom come from, Yahweh?"

"Lee, it was a manifestation of mine and it was because of the difficulty that I had creating the first atom that I caused it to explode creating a void. And from this void I made a larger more explosive gas and this gas billowed forth and it became the atmosphere of this first atomic explosion.

"And it was in reality a miniature universe, and so it gave me time to gather my thoughts and create a much larger version, as I wanted to do this. And then I became confident with my work and created all of you too."

"This void then is the opposite of a black hole, Yahweh?"

"Lee, it is and the black hole is the reverse procedure that I made recently to allow the universe to expand without problems that were taken into consideration, and I will explain this.

"Within the atom the void is in line, a dimension is on one side, and the universe is on the other. With a little movement the thin line dividing the universe from this other dimension is lessened to such an extent that they tend to merge and the resultant explosion is devastating.

"And it brings with it a vacuum and from that vacuum it creates a space. And from that space the swirling gases fly and from the coalescing gases that form, life is created.

"And from life the people are made and from people my helpers and I have made many species to watch. And we have made each species a habitat to suit. And that is the reason why so many countries are entirely different.

"And the reason is that I made each country to suit each people. And what is a paradise to you is a jungle for others and what is a freezing environment to you is home for others."

"What is this dimension on the other side of the atom, Yahweh?"

"It is the dimension that can be used to travel from one place to another in no time and the distance is also nothing as it is in the place where time and distance do not exist, for only time and distance exists for you. And the time it takes to go to another galaxy from your planet is nothing and the distance is nothing, as you will soon find out; and your scientists will realize this and your ideas will be improved, as you have now been told about it."

"Yahweh, if we could travel by space craft at the speed of light would we ever reach an outer extremity or is it like the world, no matter how far we travelled around it we wouldn't ever find the end, as a sphere has no beginning and no end?"

"It is not a rigid stop start and that thinking is not the way to look at it at all. Why think that you would be able to reach an extremity if it does not exist and if it did what would it be like?"

"Exactly, Yahweh and what would be beyond the outer extremity if we came to it?"

"It is not anything you can be told about as your understanding is too limited!"

"When did you begin to understand it then Yahweh, as you have grown with time?"

"It is a very big story and it is a very big mind that would be able to understand it. And the minds of men are limited so it is not the way to look and it is inconceivable that any could understand it, so please be satisfied with my answer."

"Yahweh, just try to explain it to me simplistically so that we can try to grasp it, little by little."

"Alright, and when I start tell me if it is too difficult and I will try to simplify it."

"Thank you Yahweh."

"The universe is made up of a unit of time as you understand it and this time is revolving at an amazing velocity and it is in the time that it takes to traverse from one galaxy to another, that it rotates.

"The universe is therefore in a state of change and it is constantly traversing backwards and forwards in a time warp. The universe becomes the last place to be, and then it becomes the first place to be and this cosmos is a constant, and it is a reality.

"The universe has a place and this place is known to be the void and this void is known to be from within the gravitational field of the known.

"And this traversing universe made up of a unit of time is therefore also a gravitational force and it is from this that it expands constantly becoming more. And from this it is able to become a huge expanse that has no beginning as it becomes its own past and from that it begins again."

"Yahweh, earlier you began by telling me you first created the universe from an explosion and then after this you made each planet individually to suit."

"Yes that is what I said. It was from a minute explosion of an atomic nature that I made this space. And from this I devised a means of creating a huge explosion which pushed the boundaries of my thoughts into a time warp. And this became a void of empty space with no solid matter; and from the coalescing gases I created the planets over billions of years.

"And this is my work, and this is the way I did it; and I did it myself, not just a random accident but with a purpose in mind; and this purpose is now you and you are here are you not?"

"Yes Yahweh; wouldn't people think that this huge explosion you caused is what is regarded by scientists as the 'Big Bang?'"

"The big bang theory is not true, as I will explain. The way the universe formed was entirely my idea and is not the result of any unregulated big bang as you have been told.

"I scheduled it to happen and it happened when I wanted it to happen. And the first sign was when I made a small planet from the gases and it condensed into a mass and solidified as it cooled down. And I got the idea to make billions of them as it was all I had to do then.

"And as I progressed, so did my ideas. Once I had the planets, I wanted to groom them and see if I could improve them and make them interesting, and from this thought came the planets now inhabited with abundant life.

"And from this thought came the planets that are stores of minerals waiting to be mined. And from this thought came the planets that can be harvested and can be utilized for purposes such as only humans can think of, and humans will eventually do this."

"So is this what we will be doing when we have everlasting life, Yahweh?"

"Yes Lee, the earth is limited and once all evil has been eliminated the people left will flourish and learn much more than they could ever learn before, not being restricted in any way.

"So therefore, the ones who study space travel will make it happen and the ones who study environmental science will make other desolate planets flourish.

"And they will become havens for hard working peoples who need to get away from the world and take a break, and this paradise is going to be soon, and this paradise is my promise."

"Yahweh, we who are to be with you in your houses and remain in spirit, or alternate between living in the physical state and the spiritual state, will we ever become anywhere near as developed as you are now?"

"Those I want to remain with me will keep on developing until they have the same abilities as I have. And I, being older will also have advanced so it will be the same as it is now. And I will always be your Father and you will always be my children."

"Will we be able to create life and planets as you do, Yahweh?"

"Yes Lee, and this is to be the ultimate goal!"

"So this is the answer, Yahweh? This is the reason for our being? When someone asks of me what is the purpose of it all, the purpose of living, I can tell them we are developing into being the same as our heavenly Father and eventually we will also be creating life and creating new things?"

"That is correct and it is what I want you to tell the others and they will see it as clearly as the noses on their faces. And they will see why all of those who are corrupt and wicked must be ruthlessly destroyed.

"And this is the reason for the resurrection and the judgment to weed out all the unworthy who would destroy, rather than create."

"Yes Yahweh, I see why you must rid the world of ruthless leaders and others who are so blatantly corrupt and lead the world into conflict, as well as rid us of all the people who are lawless."

"It will be my ultimate dream, come true, as I have dreams as you do and my life has been all about creating. And it will bring me the most wonderful feeling that it is possible for me to have, and the feeling will be of pure joy."

"Yahweh, when the people read this book and discover the plans you have for them, they should be very happy."

"I hope so Lee, as this is all I have that I feel is good enough for those I love, and I want them to have this privilege as you have just been told.

"I have been working on my plans for this day for hundreds of millions of years. And it is one of the best days I have had, telling you this and it is the ultimate story. And this book is the end of my secret; and it is the beginning of a new era and it will bring my plans closer to fruition."

"Thank you Yahweh, can we move on to more questions now?"

"Lee, I have been listening to your thoughts and you are pleased!"

"Yes, that is quite true, Yahweh!"

"Then do you think the people reading this will be pleased?"

"I hope so, Yahweh!"

"Lee, tell them then and leave all in for them to see!"

"I intended to leave it in, Yahweh."

"It makes me very happy to see this in writing and it makes me very pleased that you are writing it too!

"Let me remind you this is my messenger that I have anointed, to give these words to you.

"Let me state this authorization is my plan to let all have my word.

"Lee will give you further information over the next few years and it will be information about my future plans, concerning my Son.

"Let me remind you this is the only time Lee will be allowed to give you these details, so listen to him for your own peace of mind.

"Lee will oversee all things pertaining to my Son and he will inform all people of the happenings as they occur.

"Let me remind you this has been foretold for centuries now and it is the way, and it is my plan.

"Let me state emphatically that my plan is the final plan and not a rehearsal, but the real thing.

"Let me give you encouragement in that no faithful believer will perish in my final judgment, but will enter my house and be saved.

"Let me add that all those who are not here will be judged at the time of my Son's arrival, and this will take the 144,000 angels in heaven and on earth that you have been told about, and these messengers are disbursed throughout the world and will be the ones helping my Son. (Revelation 7: 5-8)

"Lee will help in this too and you will see him carrying out some of his duties with the angels, and you will see this very shortly too.

"Let me state that I am the God who created you, so be kind in your thinking now and do not criticize the messenger, rather look into and reflect on your own thinking.

"And reflect on your own beliefs and ask yourself if this is not why you are here reading this today. And if not, then stop reading now, as this reality is my plan.

"And if this reality is too real and too literal and too painful to face up to, then it is the wrong time for you to be here reading it; so stop reading my word now and leave this building before you are overcome with it all.

"Lee will release the information regarding the return of my Son to the media when the time is close, and he will tell the people what to look out for and where it will take place and what you are to do when this happens.

"My thoughts are with you today so be pleased you have heard my word. And this will be a taste of more to come in the near future as it is imperative you are told of these things now and not on the day it happens; and be prepared so as not to be found in a bad way, but in a way of worship in my Son's house.

"Let me remind you, this is not far off and if you dally now it will be too late to arrange for the end times as they are nearly here. And the wicked will be in charge as the devil has them in his grip.

"Let me show you firsthand that you are to be exalted, as you have not succumbed to the ways of the devil and have exonerated yourself of any sin, by asking me to forgive you, and I have.

"Let me tell you I will be here to meet you and I will embrace you as you are mine to give my love to. And this love is forever and ever, so be kind to each other and embrace each other too as it is universal love, not yours to keep but yours to share.

"And it is love that brings us together to share our thoughts, and it is love that binds you to your family, and you are my family too.

"Lee will let you have more information about me if you ask him, and it will be the first time I will divulge personal information about myself to the people I love and have created in my image.

"Let me tell you I am looking forward to the day you are all in my house enjoying my hospitality and sharing in my plans. And this life will be the best life imaginable, so look forward to it with joy and look forward to it with anticipation of a great beginning, not the end but the beginning, and this beginning is for you.

"I am letting this testament end today. And this will be the start of my communication with any of you who want more and wish to know more about me and my plans for you. Let it be seen that this testament is due to be read by millions who are looking for the truth, and this testament will provide the truth.

"My Son is the truth and to find him you must read his testament first. My messenger will tell you all you need to know to find him, and you will be guided into truth either by his personal message to you, or by reading my personal message to you.

"Let me remind you reading this testament that I will be waiting to hear your voice calling for me to let you in. And if you are willing to come into my house you will find you are in good company.

"My life will be for your comfort in here, and your life will be for your experience and your growth until you are capable of doing what you are meant to be doing. And that is creating life of your own and making planets for living beings to grow into what you are now.

"Lee is the one doing this for me and he will grow into what I am eventually and you will too, so take my word for it that this is the reason you are in existence.

"And you live and die and you see and hear in life as well as in death, unless you err in judgment and are discarded and have been bad like the leaders who are to perish, and that is to be their reward for their bad behavior.

"My life has been one of great difficulty as I have stilled my hand from striking, and my wrath has built up to the point that if released in one fell swoop it would devastate all living things as well as the rest of the universe; so I have to put my own feelings before the lives and the loves of those on earth first, as it will be the beginning of another era.

"And this will be very soon indeed as you have been told for centuries, and this is happening shortly, not hundreds of years or tens of years, but very soon.

"My Son is my throne and on him I sit. Let it be seen that he carries me in more ways than one. My Son is my universe and he will be in the universe that I made for you and he will be in charge; so be ready to be in his universe when he arrives to take you there.

"My attitude to people has changed as they are more than they were in the beginning. And they are quite capable of thinking things through now because of new found freedoms and facilities now available to most, such as libraries and computers which hold the key to many unknowns.

"And the people have had limited education for centuries, but now they know that to find information is not as daunting as it was in the not so distant past. And all have the ability to find what they need, and if not, someone near to them will help find it for them.

"Lee is doing my work on a computer now and he finds out many things by searching the Internet, so it is up to you to find me but not in that way, find me by seeking me in your heart and by seeking me in your soul.

"This will be the way to find me and if you seek long enough you will find not only me but my beloved Son who will bring you into my house. And you will be welcomed by thousands and you will be overjoyed to be among those who are good, and not evil.

"The bad souls will get their reward, and they will seek the way but it will be far too late for them and they will perish.

"And who told you I am a kind and compassionate God? Who told you that your life was going to be wonderful on earth? Who led you into thinking that you were the one to be seen as my favorite?

"Let me ask you another question now. What do you intend to do with yourself once you have gained everlasting life in my house?

"Let me tell you what you will be doing then. My angels are preparing to make several more universes and you are to prepare the planets for habitation, and you are to help design the animals and birds and higher species.

"And you will determine what their attributes will be, and you alone will feel the responsibility; and you alone will be able to determine what they will be like and what their purpose will be, and how they are to eke out a way to live; and you alone will try, though few will be able to manage without my help.

"And as for you Lee, let me tell you that I love you and you are doing what you are supposed to be doing, and that is writing my words and instructions down for all to see.

"Let me remind you that you are the one who is to give these words to the world in your own time, and your own space.

"My wish is that it be done as soon as you can do it and that it will not take much longer, as you are coping with many disruptions in your life at the moment.

"Let me say that this is my final word to the living, and all of you will find me in spirit when you die. Do not think it is hard to find me as dying is not hard. Let me tell you in this last passage that I love you and want you to be here in my arms.

"My last word to you is to strive to be here in my house with me and be kind to your neighbors. Love each other without harming either yourself or your neighbors."

Until we meet again.

Your loving Father,

Yahweh.

BIBLIOGRAPHY

NEW INTERNATIONAL VERSION: REFLECTING GOD STUDY BIBLE.
Ed's., Barker, Kenneth; Donald Burdick, et al. Grand Rapids: Zondervan
Publishing House, 1995.

THE HOLY BIBLE: NEW KING JAMES VERSION.
Nelson, Thomas. Nashville: Thomas Nelson Publishers, 1982.

www.ingramcontent.com/pod-product-compliance
Lightning Source LLC
Chambersburg PA
CBHW071417090426
42737CB00011B/1496